L. U. Reavis

The New Republic

L. U. Reavis

The New Republic

ISBN/EAN: 9783744677998

Printed in Europe, USA, Canada, Australia, Japan

Cover: Foto ©ninafisch / pixelio.de

More available books at **www.hansebooks.com**

THE NEW REPUBLIC,

OR THE

TRANSITION COMPLETE,

WITH AN

APPROACHING CHANGE OF NATIONAL EMPIRE,

BASED UPON THE COMMERCIAL AND INDUSTRIAL EXPANSION OF

THE GREAT WEST;

TOGETHER WITH HINTS ON NATIONAL SAFETY AND SOCIAL PROGRESS.

To save the Republic of our fathers in all its parts — to purify and perfect it by the struggles through which it passes — to make it wiser and better — to give it a grander and loftier mission among the nations of the earth, and to perpetuate its existence to the remotest time, is the chief end of this and future generations.

SECOND EDITION.

BY L. U. REAVIS.

ST. LOUIS:
PUBLISHED AND FOR SALE BY JOS. F. TORREY AND CO., BOOKSELLERS, FOURTH ST.
1867.

Entered according to Act of Congress, in the year 1867,

BY JOS. F. TORREY & CO.,

In the Clerk's Office of the United States District Court for the Eastern District of Missouri.

MISSOURI DEMOCRAT, PRINT.

NOTICE.

THE first edition of these pages was written the latter part of December 1866, and the first part of January, 1867. In the meantime, the current, of public thought and events touching the matter herein contained have flowed in support of its general truth.

Encouraged by many favorable notices from the press and distinguished men of the country, I resolved to recast and enlarge the little pamphlet for a second publication.

Though very brief in its character and treatment of great questions, and to many will appear extravagant in its phraseology, yet the data that furnished its foundation, and which gave birth to its ideas, are held to be correct, as they come from reliable sources. Believing that there is nothing written herein to injure the common good of all, but that every page, however feeble, is an indication of something better to the great Republic and her people, it is submitted by one who, though humble, has no selfish motive to gratify, nor no higher aspiration than that of contributing something for the good of his country and the human race; and though the work is small, it is a suggestion of a volume which will yet come from a more gifted pen.

"Go, little book, from this my solitude,
I cast thee on the waters; go thy way."
—[SOUTHEY.

ST. LOUIS, MO., *December* 1, 1867.

"I cannot believe that civilization, in its journey with the sun, will sink into endless night to gratify the ambition of the leaders of this revolt, who seek to

> 'Wade through slaughter to a throne,
> And shut the gates of mercy on mankind;'

but I have a far other and far brighter vision before my gaze. It may be but a vision, but I still cherish it. I see one vast Confederation stretching from the frozen North in one unbroken line to the glowing South, and from the wild billows of the Atlantic westward to the calmer waters of the Pacific, and I see one people, and one law, and one language, and one faith, and, over all that vast continent, the home of freedom and refuge for the oppressed of every race and of every clime."—*Extract from* JOHN BRIGHT'S *Speech on American Affairs.*

"It is, perhaps, impossible to tell what may be the exact result of this South Carolina nullification; but do what she will, conspire with many or few, I am confident that this Union of our fathers—a Union of intelligence, of freedom, of justice, of industry, of religion, of science and art, will, in the end, be stronger and richer and more glorious, renowned, and free, than it has ever been heretofore, by the necessary reaction of the crisis through which we are passing."—*Governor* YATES' *Inaugural, January*, 1861.

"I turn, from rebellion and slavery, in humble gratitude to GOD, as I behold my country at last redeemed and fixed in history, the Columbus of Nations, once in chains, but now hailed as benefactor and discoverer, who gave a new liberty to mankind. Foreign Powers already watch the scene with awe. Saints and patriots, from their home in the skies, look down with delight; and WASHINGTON, tall angel of light that he now is, who set free his own slaves, exults that the Republic which revered him as Father has followed his example."—CHARLES SUMNER.

"I feel sure that the hour has not come for this great nation to fall. This people, which has been studying to become wiser and better as it has grown older, is not so perverse or wicked enough to deserve so dreadful and severe a punishment as dissolution. This Union has not yet accomplished what good for mankind was manifestly designed by Him who appoints the seasons, and prescribes the duties of States and Empires. No, sir, if it were cast down by faction to-day, it would rise again and reappear in all its majestic proportions to-morrow. It is the only government that can stand here. Woe! woe! to the man that madly lifts his hand against it. It shall continue and endure; and men in after times shall declare that this generation, which saved the Union from such sudden and unlooked for dangers, surpassed in magnanimity even that one which laid its foundations in the eternal principles of Liberty, Justice, and Humanity."—WILLIAM. H. SEWARD.

TABLE OF CONTENTS.

	PAGE
INTRODUCTION	5
THE NEW REPUBLIC	7
THE MISSION AND END OF THE REPUBLICAN PARTY	10
THE NEW PRESIDENT	11
THE NEW CAPITAL	12
THE NEW CONSTITUTION	12
MATERIAL POWER AND PROGRESS	13
THE ATLANTIC SLOPE	16
THE MISSISSIPPI VALLEY	17
MATERIAL POWER	18
COMMERCE	19
MINERALS	30
THE AMERICAN PASTURE	32
PACIFIC SLOPE	34
SUMMING UP	36
STATISTICAL TABLE	38-39
MANUFACTURES	41
RAILROADS	41
GREAT CITIES	44
NEW YORK CITY	44
CHICAGO	45
ST. LOUIS	46
SAN FRANCISCO	49
NEW ORLEANS	50
OTHER CITIES	54
POLITICAL POWER	55

TABLE OF CONTENTS.

	PAGE
POPULATION	57
RECAPITULATION	59
THE UNION AS IT SHALL BE—Poetry	62
FUTURE OF CIVILIZATION	63
AMERICA—Poetry	69
CONSTITUTIONAL GOVERNMENT	76
NO MORE WAR	77
WHO IS THE TRUE VOTER	81
THE LABOR QUESTION	85
THE FUTURE OF THE NEGRO RACE IN AMERICA	88
TO THE YOUNG MEN OF THE REPUBLIC	91
NATIONALISM, OR PATRIOTISM	92
OUR SOCIAL DESTINY	95
ALASKA	100
RECONSTRUCTION	101
WOMAN SUFFRAGE	103
THE PACIFIC RAILWAYS	104
COL. WILLIAM GILPIN'S DESCRIPTION OF THE SOUTH PASS	105
THE GREAT BRIDGE AT ST. LOUIS	110
SPECIAL TO ST. LOUIS	119
NOTE—ST. LOUIS AND CHICAGO	123

THE NEW REPUBLIC,

OR

THE TRANSITION COMPLETE.

Man, by nature, by creation, and by miracle, stands at the head of all life on earth, and is the master-work of God. Coming forth into being, as from an oriental sleep, on the morning of creation, with the full consciousness of his dominion over the beasts and the birds, and like them instinctively taught that his wants and necessities must be satisfied by the sweat of his brow, he set about his mission on earth in Eden. Not long had he surveyed the place of his domestic habitation until his faculties, his capacities, and his ambition sought wider range, and he leaped the narrow boundaries of Eden and began the journey of man westward around the earth. From that twilight epoch in the far east has the human race wandered forth from the rising toward the setting sun, for more than one hundred centuries. Led on by patriarchs, warriors, and ambitious adventurers, whose warm hearts throbbed for the highest interest of their followers, conquest and commerce have steadily expanded and carried with them civilization, the arts and sciences.

After thousands of years of seemingly barbaric adventure, over the wilds of Asia and Africa, with here and there a distinguished but temporary growth of science, art, and industry, commerce took up her abode around the Persian Gulf and sowed the seeds of a more permanent and advanced civilization.

"Historic records, commencing with the arrival of progressive civilization at the extremity of the Mediterranean, relate from tradition the antique Empire of Bacchus, and the religion of Zoroaster on the Ganges and the Indus. The Chaldeans of the

Persian Sea followed. Fleets came from the extreme Orient into the Bengal Sea, the Persian Gulf, and the Red Sea; and caravans overland by the Oxus and the Caspian brought the camel, the horse, cattle, manufactured wool, silks, cotton, and metals, agriculture, commerce and coin. Empires extended westward along the Ganges, the Euphrates and the Nile, reached to the Mediterranean and Euxine. From Egypt, Phœnicia, and Colchis sprung European Greece. Such as progress is to-day, the same has it been for ten thousand years. It is the stream of the human race flowing from the east to the west, impelled by the same divine instinct that pervades creation. By this track comes the sun diurnally to cheer the world. Thus come the tides of men and of the waters, learning, law, religion, the plague, the small-pox, and the cholera. The sources of life and happiness—the pestilence that saddens both. It is within a belt of the earth straddling the 40th° of North latitude that the greatest mass of land surrounds the world, and where the continents most nearly approach. Within this belt, from $30°$ to $50°$, four-fifths of the human race is assembled, and here the civilized nations, of whom we possess any history, have succeeded one another, commencing at the furthest extremity of Asia and forming a zodiac towards the setting sun. This succession has flowed onward in an even course, undulating along an issothermal line, until in our time the ring is about to close around the earth's circumference by the arrival of the American nation on the coast of the Pacific which looks over into Asia."

Following this stream of the human race has been a continued expansion of commerce and civilization. From the narrow limits of the Persian Gulf commerce sought wider range in the expanded Mediterranean, where it grew and flourished for centuries, till its growth demanded more room, and it passed from the Mediterranean to the wide embrace of the Atlantic Ocean.

"Track its history, for a moment, from the earliest period. In the infancy of the world, its caravans, like gigantic silkworms, went creeping through the arid wastes of Asia and Africa, with their infinitesimal legs, and bound the human family together in those vast regions as they bind it together now.

Its colonial establishments scattered the Grecian culture all around the shores of the Mediterranean, and carried the adventurers of Tyre and Carthage to the north of Europe and the south of Africa. The walled cities of the middle ages prevented the arts and refinements of life from being trampled out of existence under the iron heel of the feudal powers. The Hans Towns were the bulwark of liberty and prosperity in the north and west of Europe for ages. The germ of the representative system sprang from the municipal franchises of the boroughs. At the revival of letters the merchant princes of Florence received the fugitive arts of Greece into their palaces. The spirit of commercial adventure produced the movement, in the fifteenth century, which carried Vasco di Gama round the Cape of Good Hope, and Columbus to America."

The discovery of America by Columbus opened the most remarkable epoch in commerce and civilization in the world's history. It not only led to the discovery of the New World, but gave to the human mind a new impulse, and developed in an extraordinary manner and in unparalleled combination, every element of known civilization and barbarism, and applied them all with the most daring energy and ambition to serve the selfish ends of nations and individuals.

The wide Atlantic and the New World became the theatre of tragedy and transition, yet "each notable deed, in government or religion, implied a whole continent of future progress and liberty." Time has rolled on, and the wide Atlantic is no longer sufficient to answer the demands of the expanding commerce, and from her shores the pioneers of land and sea are already seeking the shores and bosom of the vast Pacific Ocean to find room for their commerce, their energy, and their ambition. Thus it is, the tide of commerce has ever been westward and wider. The goal of civilization will be found when the Pacific Ocean and her shores are fully mastered by the human race.

THE NEW REPUBLIC.

It was reported of General Banks, that soon after he entered the army at the beginning of the rebellion, while standing upon Arlington Hights, in sight of Washington, with other officers of the army, and discussing the causes and consequences of the war, he pointed to the Capitol, and said: "There stands the last of the old Government; out of this struggle will come a new nation." This declaration was heralded over the country, and read the next day by millions who gave it prophetic credence. It is herein proposed to show that the late rebellion was a transition struggle, through which the nation was compelled to pass to reach a higher plane of civilization; and that it has almost completed the transition, and that in the consummation of such an eventful change, new ideas, new hopes, and new aspirations will grow in the minds of the striving millions of the Republic, which, fed and strengthened by the wonderful expansion of the commercial and industrial interests of the nation, will demand a change of national empire and a removal of the Capital from Washington to the banks of the great Mississippi. A few of the facts will be here presented, which, by succession and by combination, point to the under-life current of the Republic, as it moves in its progressive and westward career, to that maturity and strength which of right will demand the change.

Current incidents and events, pregnant with volumes of fruitful history, teach us that we live in no ordinary times. The great flood of light which modern culture has cast over the face of the world and reflected back on history, teaches us that progress is stimulated not only by the peaceful arts and industrial achievements of formal and friendly people, but that even by spoliation, which has developed new energies and devised new means, also that wars stimulate progress, have planted and invigorated nations, and that even religion, promulgated by ambition, prayer, and the sword, has given historical fame to Jerusalem, the land of Palestine, and the Saracens, no less than it has to New England and Mexico.

"The fatal dispatch that ordered fire to be opened upon Fort Sumter gave notice to the world that the era of compromise and diplomacy had ended."

The struggle which then commenced was one which the great statesmen, not only of the United States but of other lands, had long anticipated. Neither human experience nor human history had furnished any instance where political differences, growing out of great antagonistic social relations in the same government, had been disposed of without revolution. The proneness of men everywhere to cling to existing wrong with the same tenacity that they cling to truth, renders it impossible to dispose of, by legislation, great errors that grow upon nations. Therefore, it was with reasonable expectation that the Government was swiftly drifting into an internecine struggle long foreseen as an impending punishment for national sin. Any nation passing through a struggle imposed by Providence, as a scourge or chastisement for wrong-doing, may justly be said to be in a transition state. The evidence of a transition is to be seen in the fact that a nation, while passing through the struggle, casts off an old error and becomes in the future wiser and better. Chastisements and bitter experience, for individuals as well as nations, like physical exercises, if not so severe as to impair vitality, are valuable though unwelcome teachers.

That the late national struggle has worked enduring good for the Republic, however great the sacrifice, is already fast becoming evident. Not only is freedom established throughout all the land, in fact as it was in theory, but the melting away of sectional bitterness and local hatred, added to growing and expanding industry unknown before in one-half of the country, is the most gratifying evidence of endless good obtained by the passage of the Red Sea. The accumulation of wealth, the enlargement of industry, the spread of education, and the absolute guarantee of fraternal as well as political union, are fruits of the transition, more valuable than market-price can ever command. But the gain is not to be hemmed in by selfish, State and governmental lines; it is for all men. The sacrifice was made for the human race in every land, and upon the islands of the oceans. Henceforth wherever the name of the great Republic is sounded throughout the world, with it will be associated the idea of a bulwark on the side of human rights, and universal industry and education, with a lawful guarantee and protection to all. These attained and the transition complete, who will say that we have not passed a higher plane of national life? Who will say that the Republic is not stronger and made wiser and better for having undergone the sacrifice?

Nations and men, by an inherent law of progress, are compelled, as they approach riper years, to out-grow the errors contracted in infancy and early life, and those errors which are not disposed of in a legitimate and lawful way are removed by penalty and revolution.

The United States has not escaped this certain and infallible law of correction, and what she failed in due time to do by legislation, Providence has done for her by revolution. It was a heathen custom to expiate great crimes by a paramount sacrifice. Such has been the obligation imposed upon the United States by Him who "sits on the high and holy place, and sends His rains upon the just and the unjust."

The Republic having made the heathen sacrifice and having atoned for the sin of slavery, and cleansed her garments of its stain, it is now to be seen whether we are not on the threshold of a new era, pregnant with unlimited political progress and commercial expansion. Let us see with the eyes of Cassandra what is in the future.

THE MISSION AND END OF THE REPUBLICAN PARTY.

Whatever else may be said of republican governments, they ever have been and ever will be fruitful sources for the growth of political parties. No sooner will one party run its course than will another follow.

The Republican party succeeded the old Whig party, and was organized in the interest of the anti-slavery movement of the country. Its organization did not seem to be immature nor improvident, but wise and providential to the great issues and interests of the Republic. As a party opposed to slavery, and the friend and embodiment of freedom, it was at once the loyal and progressive party of the country. It elected ABRAHAM LINCOLN, and supported his administration to secure the suppression of the rebellion and the consequent preservation of the Union. As a political party, with liberty for its controlling idea, it mastered the rebellion, abolished slavery, and saved the nation; and to-day, in its broad embrace, it holds the sovereign power of the Republic.

During the great contest when principles were superficially viewed as incidents arising among the people, the Republican party was called in succession, first the Union party, after that the Radical party, but these were only accidental names, applied under contingent circumstances, and while they have full meaning they are only embodied in the great REPUBLICAN PARTY of the country.

This party, representing the great body of the American people in their devotion to freedom and loyalty, and having control of the government, will shape the political sentiment of the nation until it once more is permanently in the hands of loyal people, with constitutional guarantees for enlarged and universal liberty to all.

The Republican party will elect the next President, during whose administration the transition will be completed, and the Republic will have passed from a state of slavery and limited rights into a state of absolute liberty and equal rights.

THE NEW PRESIDENT.

In the selection of the new President it behooves the American people to select a man of large comprehension, true manhood, unbounded patriotism and devotion to the Republic—a matured statesman, who will stand out in advance of his people as a worthy executive of a great nation; for his full installment into office will be the guarantee of the safe passage of the old ship of State through the transition storms of the rebellion, the peaceful and perfect healing of the nation from all the wounds and local prejudices among the people, the complete settling up of the affairs of the old order of things, and the coming in of the new Republic.

Under the administration of this new President will be inaugurated more great movements, wise legislation for the Republic, and industrial advances by the people, than at any other time of our history or the history of the world.

The new President fully installed in office and entering upon the duties of his broad and national mission, party spirit will melt away into the great people, whose hearts will throb in unison and devotion to an all-embracing Constitution, and the common interest of a common country. This will constitute a marked step in the new Republic, an era of hope and prosperity which is sure to come beyond the dark clouds that have so long and gloomily hung over the country. There is sure to come a new dedication, when all the people, as we are told of old, will shout hallelujahs together.

THE NEW CAPITAL.

Among the many great advances that will be made under the new President will be the removal of the Capital from Washington to the banks of the Mississippi. The truth of this will be shown in other pages. The commercial expansion and multiplication of new States in the Great West, and the preponderating millions of industrious and intelligent people dwelling in the Mississippi valley, will claim its removal. In a speech made at St. Paul in 1860, Mr. Seward, in referring to the growth of the Great West, said the time was not remote when she would gather to herself the strength of the Republic, and the power would pass from the hands of the East into those of the West, and that the Capital would come to the banks of the great Mississippi. The day for this great change of national empire is at hand. Let no man be blind to the coming change. Let no American statesman be so weak as to contend that the cost of public buildings at Washington is a sufficient guarantee for the permanence of the Capital at that place. The cost in due time will weigh nothing in the balance of power. Not even a wall around the city of Washington, and a cherubim with flaming sword upon its ramparts, can keep the seat of empire from the Great West. When the time comes for the change the public mind will be up to the occasion, and fully prepared to convert the present government buildings into great and far advanced national schools; and at the new Capital rear buildings far more magnificent in splendor and proportions than any yet reared by human hands.

A NEW CONSTITUTION.

Under the new President a new Constitution will be formed for the Republic. National progress and national necessities, aided by the advanced wisdom of American statesmen, will demand a reconstruction of the fundamental and organic law, that it be adapted to the advancement of the people—a Constitution simple in its structure, plain in its meaning, and containing two fundamental ideas of government—power and liberty; power unquestionable, and liable to no false interpretation, and not misunderstood by any, and all-embracing and all-protecting to every human being who seeks shelter from tyrants and wicked men under it—a Constitution fully fitted to the advanced and eventful times in which we live. Such a Constitution will be demanded by the people of the United States, and sought for through a special national convention.

MATERIAL POWER AND PROGRESS.

The honest and intelligent citizen is always proud of his country, and feels for her welfare as he does for himself and household. For many years it has been conceded by the nations of the earth that the great Republic of the West, or the United States, was, though young, the best Government in the world, both in her political and natural advantages.

The superiority of her political system comes from its being purely republican in form, while the configuration of her territories are hemmed in by approximate latitudes, and diversified with all the natural advantages that a country can possess.

However proud the true citizen may be of the greatness of the Republic as she now is, it is evident that she is only a child, with scarcely its swaddling clothes put off, and still resting and growing in the parent arms of two vast oceans, but with a vigor and rapidity of growth unparalleled in history or experience. Each succeeding year adds prodigies of industry and enormities of wealth that baffle the genius of the statistician, the statesman, and the tax gatherer. The change is wonderful. Years ago, before the railroad, the telegraph, and the steamboat were known, it was the rule for the pioneer, with his ox-cart, his ax and hoe, to go before and build his log cabin in the wilderness, and after him the canoe and the horse mail would come. Not so now. The telegraph, steamboat, and railroad go before in rapid march; and, instead of the pioneer, with his ax and hoe and log cabin, the village is spread upon the prairie with the magic of the tented field, and the plow takes the place of the hoe. Instead of the school-house, the church, and the printing office, being, as of old, the products of half a generation, they now take their places among the institutions of advancing civilization in a month and a year. The loom and the anvil, the steam engine and the artisan, also keep pace with the advanced guards of industry and institutions.

In this connection, it may be proper to refer briefly, with introductory remarks, to the topography or general character and configuration of our continent, and draw what lesson we can for its adaptability to one government and one people over all its broad extent.

It has been a growing conviction of scientific men and philosophers that the character, homogeneousness, individuality, and nationality of the people of a country are shaped by the peculiarities and configuration of that country.

It is argued that high mountain ranges in the central part of a continent, such as in Europe and Asia, manifest a divergence in the physical aspects of the continent, as will be seen in the flow of its rivers and the layers of its stratas, and that these natural divergences imply a disintegration of the inhabitants of such countries, and the formation of different nations of people. It is argued that this truth can be traced all through the physical history of the people of Asia and Europe, and that by the formation of the continent can be mapped out the territory of the different nations that are to come upon it. This doctrine has been argued with a great deal of care and ability by Col. Wm. Gilpin, now Governor of Colorado, who has been long known as a distinguished pioneer and literary philosopher of America, whose whole mind has been for many years devoted to the study of the mountain system and physical geography and topography of our and other lands. He has in many respects been regarded as visionary, like all men in advance, but the next generation will read his writings afresh, and with just appreciation. In his great natural studies he has been the student of Humboldt.

The argument continues, that while Europe and Asia present a divergence of continent and nationality, America, owing to her mountain chains being stretched along her coasts, thus driving her rivers to the center, presents a configuration of convergence and unity by nature, and therefore securing a unity of nationality all over the continent. It is argued, in evidence of the truth of this doctrine, that the Indian tribes all over the continent present a strong similarity in character, habits, and customs, almost resembling branches of the same family, tempered by natures of consanguinity.

This doctrine has been more recently taken up by John William Draper, L.L.D., in his new work on the American war. With his vast learning and deep insight, he is enabled to look through the sciences and comprehend its truth. He, too, argues the unity of nationality over all the continent; that the mountain ranges on both sides lock arms in an indissoluble embrace across the Mississippi and her tributaries, and thus, by the sanction of Providence, make a home for one people, one law, one language, and one faith over all this vast continent.

In the consummation of this great truth, which God and man unfolds as a higher display of the wisdom of each, we must not be so selfish in our progress as to forget Columbus and Humboldt. Though their nativity was in Europe, "it is for America that they have lived; to us they belong; apostolic citizens of our destiny."

Leaving the simple statement of our national past, present, and prospective, we shall proceed at once to collate and present, in tabular form, the evidences of our nation's genius, wealth, industry, and greatness, as we can gather them from the United States census and other reliable sources.

That we may carry out and present intelligibly to the reader the object of the work, we shall divide the States and Territories into four divisions, as follows:

I. The Atlantic Slope.

II. The Mississippi Valley, from the Allegheny Mountains to the twentieth meridian of west longitude, or conforming to a line from Lake Winnipeg to the mouth of the Sabine river, will comprehend the great grain-growing district of the United States.

III. West of the line drawn between the mouth of the Sabine river and Lake Winnipeg, to the thirty-fifth meridian of west longitude, will constitute essentially the great American pasture or stock-growing region.

IV. From the thirty-fifth meridian of west longitude to the

Pacific Ocean will embody the Pacific Slope, and ultimately constitute that portion of the continent upon which will culminate American civilization—the birth-place and home of the greatest poets, seers, and scholars the world will have seen.

Having stated our four grand divisions, we shall proceed with the work before us.

	Square Miles.
The superficial area of the United States, including all her Territories and water surface of lakes and rivers, is.........	3,010,250
The area of the Atlantic Slope is...	423,197
The area of the Mississippi Valley, including American pasture, is...	1,899,811
Pacific Slope has a superficial area of.................................	627,256

These subdivisions only refer to land surface.

The subdivisions, with annexed figures just given, are the old geographical divisions of the country, made long before its commercial and industrial interests had assumed any reliable proportions, and when the white man knew but little of the Far West.

We shall only use this old division for geographical purposes, and the new division for the purpose of illustrating the future progress and development of civilization upon the continent.

THE ATLANTIC SLOPE.

The Atlantic Slope has a superficial area of 423,197 square miles, which is, with the exception of Russia, more than twice as large as any country in Europe. Its general surface is broken and mountainous, its soil is good, but has become considerably worn in many parts by long cultivation. Minerals of incalculable value are scattered throughout the extent of the Atlantic Slope; also timber of the best quality and kind is abundant in all its parts. Such are the natural advantages of this part of our common country, that it will ever be, as it now is, a first-class manufacturing and commercial region. The advantages in this respect are so great that the New England and Atlantic States will constitute the great manufacturing and commercial portion of the United States, and also the great consuming district; and, though it has less than one-third the territorial area of the Mississippi Valley, age, and its circumstantial relations to the commerce of the world, will, for generations to come, give it pre-eminence and control in commerce and manufactures on the American continent. Its vast wealth, its concentrated capital, its advanced elements of civilization, will essentially characterize and distinguish it as a part of our country. The superior natural advantages; the cheapness in industry wrought out of advanced and combined skill and capital; the improved facilities for transportation—all unite to make the Atlantic Slope a permanent home for the mechanical arts, and give to its cities the control of our foreign commerce for years to come. Its extended fisheries and vast ship-building interest will probably never be rivalled on the continent.

The Atlantic Slope comprises the following States: Connecticut, Delaware, Florida, Maine, Massachusetts, Maryland, New Jersey, New York, New Hampshire, North Carolina, Pennsylvania, Rhode Island, South Carolina, Vermont, Virginia, Georgia, and District of Columbia—17.

One-sixth of the total area of the whole United States belongs to the Atlantic Slope, and fifty-four per cent. of the whole main shore line of the water transportation facilities. Of the available river transportation, there is about one thousand miles. Of the commerce of the Atlantic Slope, it is, at present, almost the commerce of the country, and we shall speak of it in general terms elsewhere.

THE MISSISSIPPI VALLEY.

Passing westward of the Alleghany Mountains, we at once enter the Mississippi Valley, or that portion of our country drained by the Mississippi river and her tributaries. The Mississippi Valley, viewed as a whole, may be regarded as one great plain between two diverging coast ranges, elevated from 400 to 800 feet above the sea. St. Paul, the head of navigation on the Mississippi, is 800 feet above the ocean; Pittsburg, at the junction of the Monongahela and Allegheny, forming the Ohio, 699 feet; Lake Superior, on the north, 600 feet; but the watershed on the west, at South Pass, rises to nearly 7,500 feet.

It is traversed by no mountain ranges, but the surface swells into hills and ridges, and is diversified by forest and prairie.

Leaving out the vast pasture lands west of the Missouri, the soil is incomparable in fertility, is easily cultivated, and yields abundant returns. The climate is healthful and invigorating, and altogether is the most inviting to immigration of any portion of the earth.

This valley has a superficial area of 1,899,811 square miles, which is much more than twice as large as all the Atlantic States, and almost as large as all the countries in Western Europe. Within this valley is the finest body of agricultural lands in the world. Crossing westward over this valley, to the west line of Missouri, we span the great grain growing district, which will constitute and essentially embody the agricultural system of the United States. Providence has prepared it for the three greatest inland interests belonging to civilized man side by side lie the grain growing and the cotton or fabric growing regions, and immediately to the west of both of these lies the great American pasture or stock growing regions, stretching away to the mountains and from our northern boundary to the Gulf. Aside from the three great advantages just mentioned, which this valley possesses, it also abounds in inexhaustible minerals, iron, lead, coal, copper, and other valuable metals. Its immense forests and its water powers fit it for many of the valuable manufacturing pursuits, while its rivers and lakes already furnish a greater internal commerce than belongs to our sea-board cities. In short, God has made it the fittest abode for the greatest, most industrious, most intellectual, and most progressive people on the planet, and He has decreed their mission, and they must fulfill it.

MATERIAL POWER.

The Mississippi Valley includes the following States and Territories: Arkansas, Alabama, Illinois, Indiana, Iowa, Kentucky, Kansas, Louisiana, Michigan, Missouri, Mississippi, Minnesota, New Mexico, Ohio, Tennessee, Texas, Wisconsin, Nebraska, and the Territories east of the Rocky Mountains—18.

Over two-fifths of our whole national territory belongs to the Mississippi Valley, and twenty-eight per cent. of the main shore line belongs to the Gulf coast. Of the available navigation, there is belonging to the Mississippi Valley about 13,173 miles. It has the most stupendous system of internal navigation of any country, and with the least obstacles for its artificial expansion.

COMMERCE.

Of the commerce of the Valley States, much can be said. The growth of population, and the increase of surplus products, necessarily demand great and extended facilities for transportation and travel. Not only have the thousands of miles of our net-work of railroads failed to meet the wants of the public, but the demand is still greater for enlarged canal facilities. Already the valley of the Mississippi embraces a drainage area of 1,224,000 square miles, which is near one-half of the entire area of the United States.

Its navigable rivers are as follows:

Mississippi, from the Gulf of Mexico to Fort Snelling	2,131 miles
Missouri, from mouth to Bosman	3,525 "
Ohio to Pittsburg	1,036 "
Illinois to La Salle	300 "
Washita to Arkadelphia	601 "
Red River to Jefferson	720 "
Yazoo to Le Flore	257 "
Little Red to Searcey Landing	45 "
Arkansas to Fort Gibson	800 "
White to Forsyth	692 "
Black to Pocahontas	150 "
Currant to Doniphan	60 "
Tennessee to Florence	289 "
Cumberland to Nashville	193 "
Osage to Osceola	200 "
Kansas	200 "
Big Sioux	75 "
Yellow Stone	800 "
Minnesota	295 "
St. Croix	60 "
Chippeway	— "
Monongahela to Geneva (slack-water, 4 locks)	91 "
Muskingum to Dresden, do 8 do	100 "
Green River to Bowling Green do 5 do	186 "
Kentucky to Brooklyn do 5 do	117 "
Kanawha to Gauley Bridge	100 "
Wabash to La Fayette	335 "
Salt to Shepherdsville	30 "
Sondey to Louisa	25 "

NOTE —Steamboats have ascended the Des Moines to Des Moines City, Iowa River to Iowa City, Cedar River to Cedar Rapids, and the Moqueketa to Maqaketa City, but only during temporary floods. Boats have gone up many other small rivers in past years, but as the country becomes more cultivated the wash and drift is greater, and the smaller streams fill up, and are thus rendered useless for navigable purposes.

TABLE SHOWING THE DIMENSIONS OF THE FIVE GREAT AMERICAN LAKES.

These lakes constitute the greatest body of fresh water in the world. Their commerce might of itself be taken as the measure of the internal exchanges of the Northern States, east and west, adding to its quantity the greater portion of some three railroads. The shipping employed on these great lakes has had various alternations of fortune. The development of steam and sailing vessels began to be conspicuous in 1833, and rapidly rose in the succeeding five years to 50,000 tons. In 1843, another great impulse was given to that trade, and with the exception of a slight reverse in 1857, has steadily increased to the present time.

Lakes.	Greatest length in miles.	Greatest breadth in miles	Height above sea. Feet.	Area in square miles
Superior	355	160	600	32.000
Michigan	265	80	576	22.000
Huron	210	160	574	20.400
Erie	210	45	560	9.600
Ontario	160	45	235	6.300
Total				90.300

The commerce of these lakes, whose annual value reaches $450,000,000—more than twice the external commerce of the whole country—is carried on by a fleet of 1,643 vessels, of the following classes:

TABLE SHOWING THE CARRYING FLEET ON THE LAKES.

	No.	Tonnage	Value.
Steamers	143	53.522	$2,190,500
Propellers	254	70.253	3,573,300
Barks	74	33.203	982.900
Brigs	85	24.831	526.200
Schooners	1,068	227.831	5,955.550
Sloops	16	667	12.770
Barges	3	3.719	17.000
Totals	1,643	413.026	$13,257,020

TABLE SHOWING THE CONVEYING FLEET ON THE MISSISSIPPI RIVER AND ITS TRIBUTARIES.

Ports.	No. of Steamers	Registered tonnage	Carrying capacity	Value in dollars
*Cairo...........................	....	....	......	....
Cincinnati	150	30,497.16	42,983	$4,134,000
Dubuque	20	3,204.37	5,137	459,500
Evansville.....................	25	3,043.51	5,019	402,600
Galena	20	2,297.77	3,305	435,000
Keokuk	15	1,173.86	2,192	178,500
Louisville	66	14,100.64	25,425	1,994,500
Memphis	70	9,849.62	15,121	1,011,200
*New Albany.................	....	....	......	....
Nashville.......................	12	1,183.06	2,156	108,000
*Natchez........................	....	....	......	....
New Orleans.................	80	15,860.07	21,625	1,292,000
Paducah........................	10	1,100.80	2,893	265,000
Pittsburg (81 tugs).......	159	33,598.00	42,471	3,920,800
*Quincy.........................	....	....	......	....
St. Paul.........................	39	3,088.52	4,973	607,500
St. Louis.......................	210	86,532.34	110,769	8,830,000
*Vicksburg	....	....	......	....
Wheeling......................	44	9,538.11	8,075	918,000
Totals	910	216,067.83	292,144	$24,556,600

* No registration at these ports for want of local inspectors.

The number of vessels and their tonnage, now employed on these waters, as shown in the above exhibit, is much smaller than the number in use before the late rebellion. The number of barges, lighters, and similar crafts used as auxiliaries, is very large, but the enrolling of such has not been carried out.

Also, to the above list, and to the commercial interest of the country, belongs a large fleet of canal boats, a list of which we have not been able to procure.

It is proper to notice, in this connection, that an essential improvement, constituting a new era in the commercial interest of the Valley States, will soon be made. In addition to the unlimited expansion of the railroad system of the country, there will soon be developed a canal system. In no country have the railroads been able to do all the work offered them; besides, there is a universal growing demand for canals. The Mississippi river and her tributaries are feathered with smaller streams that can easily be converted into fine canals. The abundance of products, and the cheapness of freights, will necessarily demand their construction. What are the facts? Sugar is shipped from New Orleans to St. Louis at 30 cents per hundred, by boat. The same sugar, from New York, by rail, will cost $1 per hundred. Teas will cost $2 40, while the same freight can be shipped from New York, via New Orleans to St. Louis, for $1 40. Again, on examination we find that the Atlantic and Mississippi Steamship Company, of this city, and other steamboatmen, can carry freight to New Orleans from this port at $4 per ton, while the same distance by rail will cost $15 per ton.

To illustrate further: A steamer that will carry 1,000 tons of freight 1,000 miles will cost about $80,000, and to make the trip will require 75 hands and 20 days. Cost of hands and officers for round trip, about $11,000.

To carry 1,000 tons of freight 1,000 miles on railroad will require —

6 locomotives, value,	$108,000
100 cars,	120,000
Six days, for time of trip, 36 train hands, at $90 per day,	540
Total	$228,540

It will be seen by these figures that the expense of freighting by railroad, except at a distance on the Missouri river, is much higher than by steamboat; yet, even with this fact before us, there can be no impediments to the building of railroads. The canal is an intermediate means of conveyance, carrying at less rates of freight than by rail, and at longer time than by steamboat or rail. With such a prairie country as belongs to the Valley States, and the increase of products for distant markets, there will necessarily be a demand for the construction of numerous canals. In addition to this, the introduction of grain elevators, which have become so popular as a means for facilitating the handling of grain, in shipping, will necessarily (and soon) make a radical change in the structure of barges, canal, and other boats, used for shipping grain in bulk. Grain dealers and shippers will find it essential to so construct the internal arrangement of their boats as to facilitate the taking out of grain.

Again, when our political difficulties are healed, the currents of commerce will undergo many changes, and millions of bushels of grain, and as many pounds of freight, that now find their way to distant markets, will go down the Mississippi, and out at the Gulf, and thence to the different markets of the world.

We submit the following letter from the Hon. Platt Smith, of Dubuque, Iowa, to show that freights are cheaper down the Mississippi river, *via* New Orleans to New York, than by the northern route. Mr. Smith is a lawyer of shrewd observation, and well informed upon the railroad and steamboat interests of the West:

DUBUQUE, *November* 4, 1865.

I wish to call the attention of your readers, particularly those concerned in the purchase and shipment of grain, to the following facts:

The cost of shipping a bushel of wheat from—

Dubuque to Chicago is..	12 cents.
Elevators and charges in Chicago, say...............................	3 "
Freight from Chicago to Buffalo..	16 "
Charges to Buffalo..	2 "
Freight from Buffalo to New York..	25 "
Total..	58 cents.

This is not high enough, for the reason that no allowance is made for insurance; but the figures are sufficiently exact to illustrate the case which I wish to present. About 4½ cents, between Buffalo and New York, is paid as tribute to the State of New York under the name of tolls. I contend that the State of New York has no right to levy more tolls than would be sufficient to pay the interest on the canal debt, and that the excess is nothing but tribute levied on Western farmers.

The cost of shipping a bushel of wheat from—

Dubuque to St. Louis is...	12 cents.
Freight, St. Louis to New Orleans.......................................	10 "
Handling and tonnage in New Orleans............................	3 "
Freight, New Orleans to New York.....................................	8 "
Total..	33 cents.

The Mississippi river is usually open eight months in the year, and sometimes nine. All that is required to make the route *via* New Orleans feasible, is an elevator at New Orleans, and a sufficient number of good boats, to ship in bulk, to run from the Upper Mississippi to New Orleans.

As the Mississippi is usually closed about four months, and it is desirable that farmers should market their grain in the winter, they could avail themselves of the Illinois Central Railroad from here to Cairo, but of course at higher rates. I am advised by good authority that the Illinois Central Company will grant every facility necessary for the purpose of constructing elevators at Cairo. I presume that a—

Fair charge for freight to that point will be about........	25 cents.
Elevatorage, etc., at Cairo...................................	2 "
Freight, Cairo to New Orleans............................	10 "
Handling and tonnage in New Orleans..................	3 "
Freight, New Orleans to New York.......................	8 "
Total.........................	48 cents.

This is seventeen cents a bushel less than *via* Chicago.

The saving on either of the Southern routes would be added by the wharf buyers to the price paid to the farmers. Time is said to be money, and the saving of time in getting through products to market in the winter would be very great over the lake route. Buffalo harbor is usually closed for five months in the year and sometimes six.

The Mississippi is free. The State of Illinois levies tribute upon all products passing over it, whether they go from Dunleith to Chicago, or from Dunleith to Cairo. Seven per cent. of the gross railroad earnings are paid into the State treasury as a tax or tribute; but this tribute is a fraction less than two cents a bushel. If that tribute was taken off, this amount would also be added to the price which the farmer would receive for his wheat.

It is high time for our shippers and business men to take this matter in hand. It only requires a little energy and some well directed capital to make Dubuque a good grain market, and to give the farmers an additional outlet and a much higher price for their products.

I am, respectfully yours,

PLATT SMITH.

When the more Eastern States exhibit that liberality due from their people to the internal interest of the country, and thereby secure the enlargement of canals on our northern border, then freight may be carried to New York from the West as cheap as it can *via* the Mississippi river. Until those canals are enlarged the Southern route will remain the cheapest.

In further justification of this position, we quote as follows from an able lecture of the late Patrick Robb, Esq., of Dubuque, Iowa:

In 1860 the whole number of acres of improved land in all the States and Territories was 163,261,389. Of this—

Missouri contained	6,246,871
Illinois	13,254,473
Iowa	3,780,253
Wisconsin	3,746,036
Minnesota	554,397
	27,582,030

Or a fraction less than one-sixth.

The total value of crops for 1864 is estimated by the Agricultural Bureau of the Department of the Interior to have been $1,564,543,690. Of this sum—

Illinois produced	$214,488.426
Wisconsin	51,938,952
Missouri	52,996,592
Iowa	71,100,481
Minnesota	13,168,123
	$403,692,574

Or more than one-fourth of the value of the entire crops of the country. But these estimates of value are the estimated value of the various products in the States where produced.

The value of the live stock, which, on the 1st of January, 1865, was $990,876,128—

Illinois had	$116,588.288
Missouri	44,431,766
Iowa	66,572,496
Wisconsin	36,911.165
Minnesota	8,860,015
	273,363,730

Or more than one-fourth.

A juster standard by which to measure the productiveness of these States would be a comparison of the amount of their respective products, since the value is so largely affected by the distance from market.

The great staples of agriculture are wheat, corn, beef, and pork. Comparing these, we find that the total number of bushels of wheat produced in all the States and Territories in 1864, (except the cotton States, whose production was almost nominal, probably not more than one-sixth of what it was in 1860), was 160,695,823 bushels, of which—

Illinois produced	33,371.173
Missouri	3,281,514
Wisconsin	14,168,317
Iowa	12,649,807
Minnesota	2,634,975
	66,105,786

Or a fraction less than one-half.

The total number of bushels of corn produced was 530,451,403.

Illinois produced	138,356,135
Missouri	36,635,011
Wisconsin	10,087,053
Iowa	55,261,240
Minnesota	4,647,329
	244,986,768

Or nearly one-half.

The whole number of cattle and oxen, January 1, 1865, was 7,072,591.

Illinois had	978,700
Missouri	471,006
Wisconsin	388,760
Iowa	561,338
Minnesota	127,175
	2,526,979

Or more than one-third.

The total number of hogs was 13,070,887.

Illinois had	2,034,231
Missouri	988,857
Wisconsin	340,638
Iowa	1,423,567
Minnesota	109,016
	4,896,309

Or more than one-third.

The entire population of the United States in 1860 was 31,443,322.

Illinois contained	1,711,951
Iowa	711,951
Missouri	1,182,012
Minnesota	172,123
Wisconsin	775,881
	4,553,918

Or about one-seventh.

Thus it will be seen that these five States, possessing only one-seventh of all the population, and one-sixth of all the improved land, nevertheless, in 1864, produced more than one-fourth in value of the entire crop—more than one-fourth in value of all the live stock—more than one-third in number of all the cattle and hogs, and nearly one-half of all the wheat and corn grown in the United States. Here we find four and one-half millions of agriculturists, along the Upper Mississippi, producing, in a single year, from one-third to one-half of all the productions of the leading staples of an estimated value of six hundred and seventy-seven millions, fifty-six thousand two hundred and four dollars.

An examination of the statistics fully establishes the additional fact that these five States, during the years 1861, '62 and '63, shipped East 150 per cent. more corn and meal, and 25 per cent. more pork products than were exported from the entire country during the same period. These States not only supply the export wheat of the entire country, but also the export corn and pork products. The contributions, therefore, made by Illinois, Wisconsin, Missouri and Minnesota, to the exports of the United States in these three leading agricultural staples alone, are as follows:

	1860–1	1861–2	1862–3
Wheat	$48,938,780	$44,187,148	$55,647,979
Corn and meal	6,387,160	9,609,879	9,623,357
Pork products	4,687,784	10,217,281	16,424,338
Total	$60,013,724	$64,014,308	$81,695,674

The entire exports of domestic products of the United States amounted to—

1860–1.	1861–2.	1862–3.
$217,666,953	$190,699,387	$260,666,110

The average exports of the country for the three years were $222,874,183 33, and the average exports which these five States contributed in wheat, corn and pork alone was $68,575,568 66, or very nearly one-third.

In 1861, '62 and '63, the average yearly tonnage of all American vessels engaged in trans-oceanic commerce, and entering the ports of the United States, was 2,564,257 tons, and the average tonnage of all the vessels of all countries engaged in oceanic commerce, and entering the ports of the United States was 5,341,867 tons. Now, the three staples contributed by these five Upper Mississippi States to our exports were equivalent to 1,315,000 tons annually. They, therefore, not only contributed one-third in value to our entire exports, but gave employment upon the ocean to more than one-half of all our American tonnage, which was equivalent to one-fourth of all the tonnage of all nations, our own included, entering the United States, and engaged in trans-oceanic commerce. History cannot furnish a parallel.

The Agricultural Bureau, basing its calculation on past results, makes the following approximate estimate of the cereal product of the Northwest for the next four decades:

Years	Bushels.
1870	762,200,000
1880	1,219,520,000
1890	1,951,232,000
1900	3,121,970,000

We consume in this country an average of about five bushels of wheat to the inhabitant, but if necessary can get along with something less, as we have many substitutes, such as corn, rye, and buckwheat. It is estimated that our population, will be in —

1870	42,000,000
1880	56,000,000
1890	77,000,000
1900	100,000,000

Accordingly, we can use for home consumption alone of wheat in—

1870	210,000,000 bushels.
1880	280,000,000 "
1890	385,000,000 "
1900	500,000,000 "

From 1790 to 1817, breadstuffs were the chief exports of some of the New England and nearly all of the Atlantic States. Now New England produces but eleven quarts of wheat to each inhabitant, and consumes annually of agricultural productions $50,000,000 more than she produces. Pennsylvania, the first, and New York, the third among the States in the production of wheat in 1860, are now calling upon the West, the former for ten per cent. and the latter for sixty per cent. of its bread, while Ohio, so long the promise land of the emigrant, is now growing but very little more wheat than will meet the wants of a population equal to her own. Nearly every State in South America, and nearly every nation in Europe, imports agricultural products, and in 1863 the United States sent its breadstuffs to sixty different foreign markets.

Russia, the chief grain exporting country of the Old World, from 1857 to 1862 inclusive, only exported annually:

Wheat	19,897,292 bushels.
Corn	2,211,932 "

The only difficulties now preventing these States from sending their products to New York, by water, are the rapids at Rock Island and Keokuk. How to remove these obstructions so as to secure uninterrupted navigation of the Mississippi, is the question at present of all-absorbing interest to the people of the Northwest.

A glance at the commerce of the Mississippi will show how necessary it is that this work should be done immediately and effectually. Thirty years ago steamboats engaged in the river trade aggregated but a few score. Now there are over a thousand.

In 1865 the imports of St. Louis, Cincinnati, Louisville, and two or three minor Mississippi towns, were of the value of $730,000,000. As the export trade of these places was about equal to their imports, we have for the entire commerce of these points nearly $1,500,000,000. But this does not include the commerce of New Orleans, Memphis, Dubuque, and other important towns. Include the trade of these points and the aggregate value of the trade of the Mississippi, and its tributaries, the Ohio and Missouri, in 1865, was more than two thousand millions of dollars—a sum equivalent to three times the whole foreign commerce of the United States. When the Atlantic States want a harbor improved, or light-house erected, they ask Congress to undertake the work, on the ground of its national importance and common benefits. If the interests of our foreign commerce require it, the General Government, without hesitation or complaint, appropriates millions for the improvement, and calls upon the West to sustain its share of the burden. If Congress can improve harbors and build light-houses as works of national importance for a foreign commerce of $600,000,000 a year, ought it to refuse, aye, under what pretext can it refuse, to appropriate the paltry sum required for the improvement of the rapids of the Mississippi, when asked as an act of justice and relief to the Northwest, and the interests of a commerce of more than two thousand millions of dollars?

What though an uninterrupted navigation of this river should build up St. Louis to the detriment of rival cities? The questions we have met to consider are vital to us all, and cannot be narrowed down to local interests and rivalries. Chicago, Cincinnati, or St. Louis must eventually become the great center of trade for the Mississippi Valley. We want and must have this river made easily navigable without any regard to its ultimate effect upon these rival points. If St. Louis shall distance its competitors in the race, and become the controlling commercial center, it will be because her own energies and advantages, which nature has lavished upon her, entitle her to the position, and all that we shall ask of St. Louis is that she shall use her commanding position and influence in accordance with true commercial honor, for the development of the trade and resources and the general prosperity of the Northwest.

Remove these obstructions, and the producers of these States will then have a convenient and adequate outlet to the markets on our own seaboard and of Europe. They can market their grain in London and Liverpool, be successful competitors of European producers on their own soil, and eventually control the price of breadstuffs in the very center of the world's trade. In Europe land is scarce and rents ruinously high. The consequence is that our farmers who have cheap lands and mechanical labor can produce grain with profit, at figures that would ruin the European farmer. The only obstacle that prevents the Western producer from underselling, and, by successful competition, driving foreign producers from their own markets, is the want of cheap transportation. For the last five years, the average price per bushel of wheat in London and Liverpool has been $1 37 in gold, or $1 90 in our own currency. The English farmer cannot produce it at a less cost with any profit. The land is mostly held by the nobility, who exact as rental therefor 40 per cent. of the productions. Improve these Rapids, and grain can be sent from Dubuque to New Orleans for 20 cents, and thence to Liverpool for 17 cents, including cost of transhipment, thus netting our farmers at least $1 50 per bushel, and giving the power to undersell the English farmer in his own market, and eventually compel him to seek other pursuits. Wheat could be shipped from this point to New York for 33 cents per bushel by the way of New Orleans, while the average cost by present transportation from the Mississippi river to New York is 65 cents per bushel. Here is a saving of 32 cents per bushel. This, on 30,000,000 of our surplus crop of 50,000,000 bushels annually raised, would make the enormous sum of $9,600,000. Nor is it unreasonable to suppose that three-fifths of the grain and flour of these States would choose the river route, because, with uninterrupted navigation, grain will find a better market on the Mississippi than on the lake, and farmers in the eastern parts of Illinois and Wisconsin will find it to their interest to look westward to the new market thus established.

MINERALS.

Of the mineral interest of the Mississippi Valley, the two great natural sources are about Lake Superior and in Missouri. The Lake Superior mines are said to be in mountain masses, sufficient to furnish an unlimited quantity of the purest iron for all time. They occupy a belt from six to twenty-five miles wide, and about one hundred and fifty miles long; also copper in abundance is found, and comprises a large part of the Lake Superior trade.

The Missouri mines, consisting of iron, coal and lead, are probably not surpassed in the world. Of the mountains of iron, we gather, briefly, from Prof. Swallow's very able geographical report of the State of Missouri:. Shepherd Mountain is 660 feet high; its ore is magnetic and specular, containing a large per cent. of pure iron. Pilot Knob is 1,118 feet above the Mississippi; its base is 581 feet from the summit. The upper section of 141 feet is estimated to contain 14,000,000 tons of ore.

Iron Mountain is 228 feet high, and the solid contents of the cone estimated to weigh 230,000,000 tons. At a depth of 180 feet an artesian auger is still penetrating solid ore.

Lead has been discovered in more than five hundred localities. It runs through twenty counties, and intersects an area of more than 6,000 square miles. The usual yearly average of all the mines, though unskillfully worked, from 1840 to 1854, was 400,000 pounds of ore.

Coal underlies a large portion of Missouri. There are some 26,827 square miles of coal fields in the State. It is estimated that in St. Louis county there are 160 square miles of coal, and in Cooper county 60,000,000 tons. It is further estimated that it would take 3,000 years, at 100,000 tons per day, to exhaust the coal of the State. "Still larger fields open up their treasures and extend through 17 degrees of latitude, and a longitude of nearly equal measure, making an area of more than a million of square miles. They are literally stocked with gold, silver, precious stones, marble, gypsum, salt, tin, quicksilver, asphaltum, coal, iron, copper, and lead; asking only an amount of labor relatively equal to that expended on California, to yield four hundred millions per annum in gold and silver alone; and in the other minerals, which will be mined as soon as transportation is provided, at least half that sum. And these things are not merely in the possible of the far future; they are near enough to answer the exigencies of our condition. A population now of thirty millions, which, during the last half century, has doubled its numbers every $23\frac{1}{2}$ years, with all the industrial enginery and apparatus of the age at command, animated by the spirit of adventure, and spurred by the faith and hope which works wonders, will be found sufficient for the achievement of greater things than we shall need or dare predict.

"But great as the promise is in these exhaustless sources of national wealth, our reliance is not alone, nor even chiefly, in the wilderness of our new world. The States called the older of the sisterhood did, in the last census decade, increase their wealth vastly more in amount and but little less in per centage, than the comparatively new ones. Ohio, first settled 77 years ago, appreciated 136 per cent., but New Jersey and Connecticut, both two centuries under culture, enhanced their wealth in as great proportion in the same time; Pennsylvania made an increase of 96 per cent. upon her large capital of $722,000,000."

These showings, together with the countless other mineral resources of the Valley States, furnish abundant evidence of the unlimited expansion of the mineral interest.

Of the agricultural interest of the Valley States we shall not attempt to say anything. All efforts in that direction would be in vain. No calculations, no figures, could definitely approach the facts that another quarter of a century will reveal. It is sufficient to state that the unsurpassing progress of an industrious and intelligent people, in an unequaled land, is a sure guarantee for a wonderful expansion.

THE AMERICAN PASTURE.

Leaving that portion of the Mississippi valley lying between the Alleghany Mountains and the Mississippi river, or more properly the Missouri, we at once enter that vast plain of country which stretches from its banks to the base of the Rocky Mountains, east and west, and from the northern boundary of Nebraska to the Gulf, and known as the great American pasture region, which, for many years, has been noted for its vast herds of buffalo and wild horses.

This American pasture is not inferior in size to the far-famed and historic Pampas of South America, which has been so long and eminently known as the greatest stock growing country in the world. Upon this vast plain sheep are more numerous than with Chaldean shepherds, while the South American herdsman is richer, in the number of his cattle, than was the man of Uz.

The great South American Pampas extends from the Bolivian province of Chiquitor to the confines of Patagonia, and from the western margin of La Plata to the eastern slope of the Andes. It embraces an area, north and south, of 800, and east and west of 1,000 miles, making a superficial area of 800,000 square miles, and is situated between 26° and 40° of south latitude, which would correspond in size with the country lying between Atchison, Kansas, and the mouth of the Rio Grande.

This great American pasture, on account of its vast prairies, which furnish by nature, in the growth of grass, almost food enough for herds the entire year, and its lack of dense forests and navigable streams, necessarily and pre-eminently fit it for the stock growing division of the continent. It is not such a country as that to which the mechanic arts will migrate, nor will it very rapidly increase in population. These facts, in connection with the certainty of the greater portion of its lands remaining cheap for many years, clearly make it the great stock raising and wool growing region of our country. Already the work is in rapid progress; thousands of sheep of the best bloods, and also cattle and horses, are fast finding their way to that unlimited but fertile and inviting pasture. Corresponding to the rapid growth of the population and wealth of the nation, will be the increase of the herds and flocks upon these broad prairies, and before another generation takes the place of the present, millions of cattle and sheep will swarm over this great pasture, as the common stock of enterprising and industrious herdsmen, who will be continually supplying near and distant markets with fine beef and mutton, and cheese and wool, from their countless herds.

This region, when properly populated with stock, is capable of furnishing pasturage for cattle and sheep in numbers more than 2,000,000,000 of each, or nearly double the present human population of the earth.

Crossing the Missouri river and the line of the State of Missouri, we enter this great pasture, which is said to offer but little inducement for the agriculturists on account of its scarcity of timber. The facts are otherwise; the greater portion of southern Kansas offers better advantages to the stock grower and farmer, than any other equal portion of the United States. Its entire lands will average good, while the emigrant, on every other quarter section of land, can dig out of one corner of it, with but little labor, stone enough to build him a good house, and fence his farm, an advantage which is not found to any great extent in any other portion of the whole country. Besides, on entering this great pastoral region there will be found penetrating it everywhere, beautiful living streams and valuable belts of timber, which, combined with high latitudes and it's genial climate, with the certainty of its interior deficiency of water and navigation being amply and absolutely overcome by artesian wells, and railroads crossing in every direction in search of new markets, will render it one of the most available and therefore productive portions of the American continent.

As the mechanical and agricultural pursuits expand in that portion of the continent lying east of the Mississippi, the stock growing business will increase west of it.

It is proper to notice in this connection, that in the future growth and dense population of our continent, the great future in the stock growing of the country will be confined mostly to the raising of cattle and sheep, as the horse is only required for his service; his raising will be confined to those who need him; the dog will soon pass away, and when the people get truly civilized, the hog will go too. The hog ought never to have been eaten, and is fit for nothing; the double use to which the cattle and the sheep can serve in furnishing food, and skins for boots, shoes, and other uses, and the wool for clothing, will ever make them valuable to man, and render their growth the more important. To this great pasture we may look more, and almost wholly, for the culture and growth of the cattle and sheep.

THE PACIFIC SLOPE.

Leaving the Mississippi Valley, we pass westward to the Pacific Slope, and into the great mountain system of our continent. It is large, magnificent, grand, and epical. It is the last step in American progress, the consecrated home of poetry.

The Pacific Slope has a superficial area of 627,256 square miles, which is more than twice as large as the Atlantic Slope. It embraces the States of California and Oregon, and the Territories of Arizona, Idaho, Nevada, Utah, and Washington—7.

One-fourth of the area total of our national territory belongs to the Pacific Slope, and eighteen per cent. of our main shore line, together with about 2,500 miles of river navigation. This portion of the country is favored with the great mountain chains and beautiful valleys, and untold wealth of precious metals. No country in the world has such strong natural characteristics combined together — its minerals, its mountains, and its fertile valleys with varied climate. In territory it is large enough for a great nation, yet it does not have one inhabitant to the square mile. This country will always be noted for its universal developments. It will be rich in agriculture, commerce, and stock-growing. It is rich in minerals. It is much larger than the Atlantic Slope. At no distant day it will be the finest sheep-growing region on the continent, and more noted for its shepherds than the mountain regions of Chaldea, where the shepherds and magi watched the flocks and the stars by night.

California and Utah already show a wonderful growth of wool, also of wine. The Pacific Slope has given evidence of its superiority as a grape-growing and wine country; its wines are highly prized in the best markets. Its mineral wealth, since its discovery, has been the magnet of the world, drawing, by its golden influence, to its shores, a thousand ships from every ocean around the globe.

When we look forward to the great changes in the commercial currents of the center of the Mississippi Valley, we must not forget that even greater will take place on the Pacific Slope as soon as the continent is spanned by a railroad.

It is difficult to say too much of the future progress of the industrial and commercial pursuits of that golden region. Yet its grandest growth will be in its future civilization, as we shall point out. In like manner, as it is the golden land by nature, so it will be the golden land in progress — the place of ultimation and culmination of American civilization.

Having briefly represented the grand divisions of our country in their respective relations and conditions, we now recapitulate with a brief survey of the whole country, its present development and future growth. In doing this it is the design to speak of every part as it relates to the whole, and indicate the centers of power and progress as current events and truth will seem to warrant, and not be partial or prejudicial to any portion. We therefore take another step forward, and behold the work of our great future advancement.

SUMMING UP.

It is estimated that over two-fifths of our national territory is drained by the Mississippi river and its tributaries, and more than one-half is embraced by what may be called its middle region, one-fourth of its total area belongs to the Pacific, and one-sixth to the Atlantic proper, one twenty-sixth to the Lakes, one-ninth to the Gulf, or one-third to the Atlantic, including the Lakes and the Gulf.

In reference to the facilities for water transportation, a calculation was made at the office of the Coast Survey, for 1853, which gives for the total main shore line of the United States, exclusive of Sounds, Islands, etc., twelve thousand miles, of which fifty-four per cent. belongs to the Atlantic coast, eighteen to the Pacific, and twenty-eight to the Gulf coast; and that if all these be followed, and the rivers entered to the head of tide water, the total line would be extended to 33,069 miles. Of the available river navigation, there is about a thousand miles respectively belonging to the Pacific and Atlantic Slopes, and about ten thousand miles to the Mississippi Valley.

Taking the continent as a whole, from the Atlantic to the Pacific, and from our northern boundary to the Gulf, it is not equaled in natural advantages by any country on the globe, and none other is more calculated to facilitate the advancement of civilization. Its immense navigable advantages, its dense forests of every variety of valuable timber, its outstretching expanse of fertile lands, and its inexhaustible and incalculable minerals, combine to make it the greatest nation of the earth in commerce, agriculture, mechanics, and wealth. In support of this statement, let us appeal to facts, and then see, after a careful examination, if we can judge anything of the future by the past.

Turning for a moment from the physical aspect of our country, we will briefly examine its present condition in the light of civilization, and draw whatever conclusions seem to be most warranted by the facts. Appealing to the United States census as the most elaborate and reliable array of facts, we shall present a condensed tabular statement, classified according to the old geographical divisions of the country, and thereby show the growth of each division, and its capacities. Taking for a basis the census reports of 1850 and 1860, we herewith submit a table, or statement, showing the material growth of the country at those dates, and also the respective growth of the Atlantic Slope, the Mississippi Valley, and the Pacific Slope.

In presenting this table, we claim for it a superiority over any tabular statement of the material growth of the country that has ever appeared in public print. It contains upon its condensed surface the growth of centuries, and materials for volumes. At one glance the eye can scan the extent of territory, the population, the wealth, the industry, the live stock, the grains, the railroads, the progress, and the great working, moving, embodiment of the country. Here, in one view, we can behold the growth of the most promising nation the world ever saw. Such is the progress exhibited, that the growth of each ten years is equal to the growth of a nation. There is no parallel in history or experience for what we are, and none will ever surpass what we will be. Let us but labor to be as good as we will be great, and the solution of the problem of man's utility upon the earth will be solved before the close of another century.

We must comprehend that with the growth of the Republic must be the intellectual and moral growth of the people. As the nation expands, so must the legislative and moral mind expand to comprehend its demands and necessities. The legislator must comprehend that the laws are yet to be of broader significance, and the moralist and the educationalist must also learn that precept and discipline must extend beyond to broader fields of use than heretofore; and may we not hope that, at no distant day, some genius may arise who will add to the material statistics of the country the statistical growth of the morals and intellectual advancement of our people, and thus furnish the measure of our most valued growth?

38 THE NEW REPUBLIC.

STATISTICAL TABLE,

Prepared from United States Census Reports, showing the Controlling Power and Progress of the Mississippi Valley.

DESCRIPTION OF RESOURCES.	ATLANTIC SLOPE.		MISSISSIPPI VALLEY.		PACIFIC SLOPE.	
	1850.	1860.	1850.	1860.	1850.	1860.
Population	13,255,254	15,903,802	9,813,117	14,993,427	107,271	491,153
Area, square miles	423,197	423,197	1,899,811	1,899,811	627,256	627,256
Land improved in farms, acres	63,965,491	73,882,853	48,885,479	87,034,199	181,644	3,537,668
Land unimp'd in farms, acres	84,508,954	93,679,468	90,736,948	142,567,264	4,191,998	7,763,090
Cash value of farms	$1,991,509,378	$3,132,361,500	$1,232,941,038	$3,446,702,533	$6,033,010	$67,780,934
Value of farming implements and machinery	$78,826,805	$105,820,439	$72,389,639	$134,292,513	$371,194	$3,985,091
Live Stock, Horses	1,441,447	2,054,269	2,460,078	3,987,645	32,194	207,260
" Asses and Mules	760,785	270,187	396,128	641,056	2,411	5,805
" Milch Cows	3,435,181	3,194,557	2,931,345	4,450,022	18,568	281,151
" Working Oxen	816,236	755,084	866,348	1,393,995	18,160	45,832
" Other Cattle	4,619,672	4,545,308	5,372,321	9,099,605	280,276	1,075,314
" Sheep	10,663,775	8,704,355	11,013,228	12,644,001	36,218	1,221,919
" Swine	10,107,505	9,767,182	20,152,783	23,254,291	33,925	554,672
Value of Live Stock	$280,479,888	$502,975,639	$257,926,413	$617,616,940	$5,774,215	$14,325,528
Wheat, bushels	47,630,178	53,306,897	48,474,581	102,057,361	836,973	7,229,988
Rye, bushels	12,803,283	15,287,195	1,382,214	4,958,375	316	65,844
Indian Corn, bushels	180,029,595	201,638,663	359,912,515	636,456,595	25,053	682,486
Oats, bushels	82,805,111	98,216,624	63,656,947	72,350,255	72,114	2,130,306
Rice, pounds	205,439,416	179,427,085	9,874,081	7,730,807		2,140
Tobacco, pounds	94,102,203	215,472,069	105,646,057	218,732,827	1,395	3,565
Ginned Cotton, bls. 400 lbs. each	899,615	1,278,646	1,546,178	4,108,270		136
Wool, pounds	27,881,509	26,502,154	24,581,022	30,765,734	44,428	2,997,035
Peas and Beans, bushels	5,696,433	8,585,405	3,514,321	6,263,209	9,147	213,381
Irish Potatoes, bushels	46,906,072	69,996,473	19,016,138	39,749,331	144,586	2,403,063

Item					
Sweet Potatoes, bushels	19,834,295	21,391,242	19,432,803	20,488,724	214,860
Barley, bushels	4,216,763	6,169,419	928,741	5,258,605	4,457,867
Buckwheat, bushels	7,111,170	13,012,306	1,539,101	4,180,396	80,411
Value of orchard products	$5,208,494	$10,637,206	$2,435,701	$8,072,064	$1,262,615
Wine, gallons	73,861	356,645	89,333	1,081,197	249,360
Value of market garden products	$3,805,066	$10,261,210	$1,285,580	$4,584,374	$1,273,904
Butter, pounds	200,161,424	257,882,960	111,968,204	167,217,182	4,552,630
Cheese, pounds	80,042,817	73,239,325	25,124,948	28,920,068	4,524,545
Hay, tons	10,213,398	10,836,040	3,308,028	6,822,187	359,769
Clover Seed, bushels	316,945	555,224	152,027	180,331	1,533
Grass Seed, bushels	300,226	282,184	116,583	563,227	4,629
Hops, pounds	3,291,549	10,148,740	205,422	252,014	1,162
Hemp, dew rotted, tons	232	301	32,961	52,979	1
Hemp, water rotted, tons	57	76	1,621	3,788	114
Hemp, other prepared, tons				13,660	
Flax, pounds	3,355,485	2,622,285	4,343,041	2,093,355	4,505
Flaxseed, bushels	213,140	142,130	349,067	424,608	69
Silk Cocoons, pounds	4,855	1,172	6,088	10,772	
Maple Sugar, pounds	22,577,904	28,030,706	11,675,532	11,989,699	1,190
Cane Sugar, hhds. 1000 lbs. each	3,673	3,072	233,141	227,910	5
Molasses, gallons, in 1850	760,030		11,940,879		
Cane Molasses, gallons, in 1860		1,005,600		13,968,390	
Maple " " "		484,378		1,277,770	82
Sorghum " " "		575,372		6,056,909	46
Beeswax, pounds, 1860		539,633		721,827	26,342
Honey, pounds, 1860		10,330,970		12,541,339	1,327
Beeswax and Honey in 1850	5,944,794		8,908,986		18,353
Value of home made manufac's	$18,100,123	$8,414,632	$16,525,229	$15,739,436	$402,788
Val. of animals slaughtered	$60,799,400	$92,478,822	$50,564,074	$115,818,366	$4,433,441
Val. of agric'l impl'ts produced	$4,639,844	$8,903,815	$2,202,767	$8,883,594	$15,205
Val. of flour and meal produced	$88,151,908	$113,196,213	$45,857,506	$103,851,894	$6,096,262
Val. of lumber sawed & planed	$37,134,449	$46,752,976	$19,037,922	$42,987,879	$6,171,431
Val. of iron foundings	$15,340,012	$21,884,915	$4,771,505	$6,061,741	
Railroads—miles of	6,948	15,345	1,641	16,174	74
R. R.—miles of, built in 10 yrs.		8,897		13,533	74

(Columns include $1,888,332 and $2,349,605 entries associated with Val. of flour and meal produced and Val. of lumber sawed & planed rows.)

By reference to the tabular statement, showing the material growth of the whole country, from the Atlantic to the Pacific, it will be seen that in 1850 the States of the Atlantic Slope were in advance of the Valley States in almost every practical and available interest belonging to the agricultural pursuits. Corn and wheat were the two principal products in which the Valley States excelled at that time. The Atlantic States had more land under cultivation, and a greater number of improved farms, the cash value of which was far greater than that of the Valley States; but the progress of ten years shows a wonderful change. When we compare the growth of 1850 with that of 1860, the advance is like the growth of a continent.

In 1850 the aggregate of improved lands in the Atlantic States was 63,965,491 acres, at a cash value of $1,991,599,378. In the Valley States the aggregate improved lands was 48,885,479 acres, at a cash value of $1,232,941,038. In 1860 the aggregate of improved lands in the Atlantic States was 73,882,853 acres, at a cash value of $3,132,561,500. In the Valley States the aggregate of improved land was 87,034,199 acres, at a cash value of $3,446,702,533, showing, in the space of ten years, an advance of the Valley States over the Atlantic States, of 13,151,346 acres of improved land, and a preponderance of cash value to the amount of $314,141,053.

In addition to this wonderful growth of the West, the States and Territories of the Pacific Slope have advanced from 181,644 acres of improved land in 1850, at a cash value of $6,033,010, to 5,587,668 acres of improved land in 1860, at a cash value of $67,780,934. These figures are most gratifying in their showing. The whole growth of the West, in agricultural pursuits, is unparalleled in the history of the human race, and yet the Republic is in its infancy. Massachusetts has but little more than one-half her acres under cultivation, while Illinois has far less than one-half her lands in farms. The improvements of the other States, in all the kindred elements of agriculture, are about the same ratio. But what are these half developments when compared with the full growth of the country? The territory of the Valley States is more than three times as large as that of the Atlantic States, and with its incomparable advantages for agriculture, must lead the way in the pursuit of husbandry.

MANUFACTURING.

While it is true that to the West belongs the great agricultural interests of the country, it is also true that to the East, or Atlantic States, belongs the manufacturing interest. The East is yet the great brain and bee-hive of the Republic. Age, wealth, and natural advantages have given to those States the capacity, and made them the home of the mechanic arts. We need only refer to the census reports for conclusive evidence upon this point. In fact, it is universally known that the Manchesters, the Birminghams, and the Sheffields, of the New World, belong to New England, and other portions of the Atlantic Slope, and to those districts of the country will they continue to belong.

The whole people are ready to adopt that policy of industrial organization that confers profits and advantages on all parts of the country.

It has long since been conceded that, owing to the largeness of the nation, the trade, the industry, and pursuits of the people must be diversified, in order to be profitable to all. The adaptability of each portion of the country to certain leading interests aids in the classification of the pursuits. Each portion has been considered in relation to some leading branch of industry: New England and the Atlantic States, on account of their immense advantages for manufacturing rather than for the agricultural pursuits, have been recognized as the manufacturing and commercial districts, while the Mississippi Valley, with its superior soil and natural agricultural advantages, legitimately becomes the great grain growing and stock raising portion; and the Pacific Slope, with mountain system and varied and picturesque country, will, in due time, open up a new manifestation of commercial, social, and civil progress, which will, in its character, be purely American.

RAILROADS.

"There are, perhaps, few or no better meters of the solid progress of nations than are to be found in the increase of railways and telegraphs within their limits. Rude and uncivilized people reject both. Just in proportion as civilization enlarges, both grow, and as business increases these indications of its increase are multiplied. While an advance is being made, the rails and wires stretch forward; when progress is stopped, these stop; and they are not only indications of progress, but they are means and adjuncts as well. They help that growth which other causes conspire to create, and convey forward the interests which they were originally designed to subserve."

Of the growth of railroads in the world, it is carefully reported that Europe has 50,117 miles of rail, Asia, 3,660; South America has about 4,000 miles of rail, and the United States had, in 1864, 49,632 miles of railroad, constructed at a cost of $1,265,962,215. There is probably an equal number of miles of telegraph to that of railroads.

Although these figures are large, our railroad system has not half reached its full expansion. The capital stock of the London and Northwestern Railway is said to be $165,000,000, and is the wealthiest in the world. The capital of the Pennsylvania Central Railway is $45,000,000, and is the wealthiest railway company in the United States. At the progress of this wonderful element of material civilization, those who stop to think may well be astonished, and their astonishment will be mingled with interest and hope on reading the following scrap of history, which we clipped from a late number of Appleton's Railway Guide:

FIFTY YEARS AGO.—Nothing shows more vividly the current events than a retrospective glance. Who can look back for the last half century, and compare the population of cities in the United States then and now, and the rapid development of steam navigation (then just discovered), to say nothing of the marvelous growth of manufactures, the vast works of internal improvement, the immense net-work of railways connecting every part of the country with each other, the electric telegraph, by which we are brought into daily communication with the Old World, including even Asia—without being struck with wonder and amazement at the speed with which we have been moving? We well remember that sterling publication, *Niles' Register*, issued weekly in Baltimore, from 1816 to 1827, by the venerable Hezekiah Niles, than whom the press never had a worthier or more genial representative. A few random passages like the following, from one of its early volumes, will amuse the curious:

"Steamships! A project is on foot in New York to build a vessel of three hundred and fifty tons, to be propelled by steam, to serve as a packet between that city and Charleston, South Carolina, in which it is estimated the passage will be made in four days! Those whose opinions are entitled to the fullest confidence decidedly believe that the voyage may be made with at least as much safety as in any other vessel."

Again, we read, as an item of interesting news, what must provoke a smile in these days:

"A steamboat has been very successfully employed in towing vessels up the Mississippi to New Orleans, at the rate of *two miles an hour* against the current and wind."

Mr. Niles speaks of a prophecy as even then fulfilling, which he heard made twenty years before, by that most ingenious man, Oliver Evans, who disputed with Robert Fulton the honor of discovering the application of steam to propelling purposes. He invented many useful machines which have since come into use, but was generally looked upon as a crack-brained enthusiast. In reply to a gentleman who expressed an opinion that the power of steam was difficult to obtain, and too troublesome to manage to be applied to useful purposes, Mr. Evans said: "Of steam, sir, we know little as yet, but that it has a power; but we shall manage it by and by with so much simplicity that the women will use it for the common purposes of housewifery—they will wash their clothes with it." It is not strange that, in that day, the idea of a *steam laundry* was considered the offspring of a disordered brain. Mr. E. added: "I believe the man is now living that will see the Ohio and Mississippi covered with steamboats—and the child is born that will travel from Boston to Philadelphia in a steam wagon in one day of twenty-four hours." The company exchanged glances of pity that genius should be so nearly allied to madness.

From the same volume of the *Register* we learn that the population of the *Territory* of Indiana was 68,084, and the editor, in surprise, exclaims: "No doubt the people will soon claim the right of being admitted as a State!" The population, according to the census of 1860, was 1,350,428.

Mr. Niles gives the population of Cincinnati in 1815 as follows: "Free white males above twenty-one years of age, 1,045; other white persons of both sexes, 5,206; blacks and mulattoes, 247—total, 6,498." In 1860 its population was 161,044.

Little dreaming of what the next fifty years would bring forth, the veteran editor remarks: "We already flatter ourselves that at no distant period the communication between Buffalo and Detroit will be as regular, and almost as expeditious, as it is now between Albany and New York." At that time Buffalo was but an inconsiderable village, its population in 1825 being little more than 2,000, though giving promise to the far-seeing of future commercial sovereignty over the vast region which lies about her. It is now the center of eight lines of railway, radiating toward every point of the compass, and noisy with the bustle of 100,000 busy human beings. Near where the city of Buffalo stands, in the year 1679, the Chevalier de La Salle built a little vessel called the "Griffin," having obtained permission from the Indians to do so. This craft was the first vessel propelled by sails that ever floated on the inland lakes. In 1862 there arrived at and departed from the port of Buffalo, 16,390 vessels, having an aggregate tonnage of 6,689,191 tons, and employing 166,133 seamen!

GREAT CITIES.

With the development of the whole country and its commerce, will also come the development of commercial centers, or great cities, monopolizing and controlling the trade of the country. Geographical conditions, and the inevitable tendency of the future commerce of the United States and the world, point to New York, San Francisco, Chicago, St. Louis, and New Orleans, as destined to be the great depots and *entrepots* for the external and internal commerce, seeking markets to and from this country.

NEW YORK CITY.

New York, as she is now, will remain a great American city; but with the civilized growth of the continent, and the change of commerce, she will be shorn of her controlling influence and leading greatness. The completion of two great internal works—the Pacific railroad to California, and the ship canal from Chicago to La Salle—will change the internal and foreign commerce of the country, and divide between New Orleans and San Francisco one-half the trade that would otherwise go to New York. As already noticed, freights *via* New Orleans to foreign or distant markets, are less than by New York, while teas, for which we pay $1 50 per pound in our markets, cost the producer 10 cents per pound, and to-day teas are more than 50 per cent. cheaper in San Francisco than in New York city. With these disparities of freights in favor of New Orleans and

San Francisco, in connection with the internal development of the country, and the classification and appropriation of every part of our soil to its proper use, we have but to override facts when we say that the Great West and her cities are not destined to control the commerce of the country, and out-number in population the cities of the East.

CHICAGO.

Chicago, aided by her bracing climate and lake atmosphere, and extraordinarily favored in her geographical position, and with a spirit of industry and enterprise unequaled in the world, will forever be a great progressive and commercial city. She may justly be called the busy Tyre of the New World.

Chicago being one of the commercial centers of the Northwest, it is proper that some space should be devoted to her commerce.

The total value of imports at Chicago in 1855	$196,660,064 66
Total value of exports from Chicago in 1855	212,953,021 88
	$409,613,086 54

The value of imports into Chicago in 1860, as per Board of Trade report, was	$97,067,616 89
Value of exports for same period	72,713,957 24
Aggregate value of imports and exports	$169,781,574 13

The value of the imports into Chicago in 1858, as reported by Col. Graham (Senate Doc., part 3, pp. 890, 891, 36th Congress, 1st session,) to the United States Government, was	$99,032,362 12
Value of exports for same period	81,052,420 05
Aggregate value of imports and exports	$180,084,782 17

The apparent deficiency in 1860, as compared with 1858, is doubtless owing to the fact that the valuation of the articles is placed higher in Colonel Graham's report than the same articles are valued by the Board of Trade in 1860, as the quantities received and shipped in the latter year greatly exceeds, in most cases, those of 1858.

It is believed that the valuation of receipts and shipments in 1861 greatly exceeded that of the commerce of 1860, (although the prices of produce are lower), inasmuch as the rebellion has diverted to Chicago an immense trade which was formerly concentrated at St. Louis, Cairo, New Orleans, and other points on the Mississippi river.

The following table, prepared by Seth Catlin, Esq., Secretary of the Board of Trade, shows the capacity of the Chicago elevating warehouses for handling and storing grains, November 15, 1861:

Capacity for storage, bushels..6,115,000
Capacity to receive and ship per day, bushels............................ 735,000
Capacity to ship per day, bushels...2,035,000

She is now the greatest railroad depot in the world, also the greatest grain depot and live stock and lumber market in the world, and, situated on the great lakes, her people will ever present the highest form of commercial industry of any people on the continent. It is a truth wrought out by physical geography, by experience, that nations or people living along great water formations, such as lakes, bays, gulfs, and inlets are more noted for commercial industry and longevity than those living on any other part of the earth. In this, the inhabitants skirting from Omaha to the mouth of the St. Lawrence have superior advantages over any other part of our country in the more enterprising and sturdy pursuits of life. This is an unconquerable advantage to Chicago.

ST. LOUIS.

St. Louis, occupying substantially the geographical and commercial center of the country, and in the heart of the richest agricultural and mineral lands on the continent, is destined to be the great central depot of the United States, and the seat of the national empire. She is the Babylon of the New World, not standing on the Euphrates, but upon the banks of the great Mississippi.

The growth and destiny of St. Louis is identical with the growth and destiny of Missouri, which is identical with the growth and destiny of the Republic. A kind of fatality has followed Missouri all the way from her territorial infancy, mysteriously allying her fate with the fate of the Republic. Hitherto, she has been the ill-fated child, causing more trouble in the national family than any other member of it,

"But now she wears her olive crown."

It must be conceded that Missouri, with her vast mineral resources, her immense forests of valuable timber, her surroundings, and penetration of commercial channels, her vast and deep-laid coal fields, her rich soil and bountiful supply of good water, for all industrial uses, stands pre-eminent as the State for diversity of civilized interests, and destined to be the home of a great and wealthy people. These things all tend to make St. Louis a great American city, destined to tread the courtly walks of commercial supremacy.

Some years ago, when the Hon. Horace Greeley began his journey across the plains, in a letter to the *New York Tribune*, from Chicago, speaking of her future greatness, he said that the child was then born that would see her a city of 1,000,000 inhabitants. Prof. Waterhouse, in his celebrated letters to the *New York Tribune*, upon St. Louis and Missouri, said that at the end of this century St. Louis would be a city of 1,000,000 inhabitants.

Touching the future of St. Louis and Chicago, and also New Orleans, and the thousand other growing cities intervening is the construction of what is termed the Ship Canal, or the enlargement of the Michigan and Illinois Canal, and the improvement of the Illinois river, so as to admit of the passage of large steam, sea-going vessels. This work once completed, and it must be soon, even if Illinois and Missouri are compelled to build it, would open up an internal commerce through the country, grander and of greater magnitude than the most sanguine expectant can conceive of.

Contemplate the construction of this great commercial artery, by which to afford the elaborate system of continental transportation—contemplate an army of commodious freighting vessels moving through the heart of our continent like great amphibious monsters of a new era—contemplate more than double the present population of our States along this great commercial channel, and more than double the surplus yield of staple products seeking foreign markets at the opening of spring navigation—contemplate a well regulated system of industry controlling and guiding every citizen in the great struggle for peace and plenty, and prompting each in demanding profits for his or her labor—then will we not begin to realize the approach of the real growth of the Great West and her cities.

Touching this great work of the West, we quote from the great statesman of Missouri, Thomas H. Benton, a man whose vast information and ideas were worthy of the Mississippi Valley. In 1847 he addressed the River and Harbor Convention in words worthy of being recalled to the attention of the American people to-day. He says:

"The lake and river navigation of the Great West, to promote which your Convention is called, very early had a share of my attention, and I never had a doubt of the constitutionality or expediency of bringing that navigation within the circle of internal improvements, by the Federal Government, when the object of the improvement should be of general and national importance.

"The junction of the two great systems of waters which occupy so much of our country, the Northern lakes on the one hand, and the Mississippi river and its tributaries on the other, appeared to me to be an object of that character, and *Chicago the proper point for effecting the union;* and near thirty years ago I wrote and published articles in a St. Louis paper in favor of that object, indicated and almost accomplished by nature herself, and wanting from man little to complete it. These were probably the first formal communications upon authentic data in favor of the Chicago canal.

"The nationality of the Chicago canal and the harbor at its mouth are by no means new conceptions with me.

"The river navigation of the Great West is the most wonderful on the globe, and since the application of steam power to the propulsion of vessels, possesses the essential qualities of open navigation. Speed, distance, cheapness, magnitude of cargoes, are all there, and without the perils of the sea from storms and enemies. The steamboat is the ship of the river, and finds in the Mississippi and its tributaries the amplest theater for the diffusion and the display of its power. Wonderful river! Connected with seas by the head and by the mouth, stretching its arms toward the Atlantic and the Pacific—lying in a valley which is a valley from the Gulf of Mexico to Hudson's Bay—drawing its first waters not from rugged mountains, but from the plateau of the Lakes in the center of the continent, and in communication with the sources of the St. Lawrence and the streams which take their course north to Hudson's Bay—draining the largest extent of richest land, collecting the products of every clime, even the frigid, to bear the whole to market in the sunny South, and there to meet the products of the entire world. Such is the Mississippi. And who can calculate the aggregate of its advantages and the magnitude of its future commercial results?"

SAN FRANCISCO.

It is highly probable that San Francisco will be the great coast city of the Pacific Slope, notwithstanding at the mouth of the Columbia river is a better harbor, and also the table lands lying upon it are far superior for agricultual purposes than those around San Francisco. So says Col. Wm. Gilpin, in his valuable work entitled "The Central Gold Region." The Pacific Slope, however, furnishes ample room for at least four great coast cities—one in Lower California (or on the Gulf of California), San Francisco, Astoria, and the fourth on the Georgian Gulf. Time will develop on the Pacific coast four great cities, but the present condition of things give San Francisco the advantage, and she will no doubt retain it for generations to come. My present purpose is, then, to point to her as the great seaboard city of the Pacific Slope. Her future will be both marvelous and great—marvelous, because she is the commercial center of a wonderful country; great, because she is destined to be the depot through which two-thirds of our foreign commerce is to come.

The diversity of our soil and climate and the expansion of our industry will soon lessen our demand for foreign goods. This will cut short our trade with approximate foreign nations, and compel our vessels to go to Asia and other ports of the Orient for silks, perfumes, gums, precious stones, and other rare articles of China, Japan, and Turkey. This will transfer most of our foreign commerce to the Pacific Ocean, thus making San Francisco the great point for the import of foreign goods.

The construction of one or more great railways to the Pacific Ocean will be the greatest miracle of our continental progress; it will be the completion of the great artery of civilization and commerce around the world. Thus, man can make the circuit of the globe by steam, and draw the distant nations nearer. What millions are waiting, and what results are depending, upon the completion of this great work! By the census of 1860, our wheat and corn crop amounted to the value of $1,000,870,990. Of this amount, a vast deal of it must find a foreign market. Fronting our Atlantic Slope, we have 205,000,000 Europeans who almost feed themselves. Fronting our

Pacific Slope, we have 745,000,000 of hungry Asiatics and Polynesians, who have spices, porcelain, and other valuable commodities to exchange for our food. From San Francisco and Astoria these millions of consumers may be reached directly, over a tranquil ocean and under a temperate atmosphere. With the completion of these great railways across the continent will open a new era in the commerce and growth of the great West, and San Francisco will balance New York, with St. Louis in the center, Chicago north, and New Orleans south.

NEW ORLEANS.

In discussing the present and future of New Orleans, I feel that I have under consideration an American city that is destined to be the most populous and princely city in the world. Providence has so ordained it, and man must build it.

Slavery has, for many years, stifled the growth of New Orleans; but now the incubus is removed. She is left to her advantages. Situated at the mouth of the Mississippi river, and upon the threshold of the Gulf, with a great undeveloped commerce above her, which must, in due time, find its way through her markets, and great tropical countries, rich in all the fruits and products of those prolific regions, just before her, she is destined to become the greatest city in the world. She ought to have been, to-day, the greatest on the Western continent.

In considering her future growth to that of the first metropolis of the world, within the first half of the next century, we are not to be guided in our calculations by the present tendency of commerce in its expansion over the continent. We are to look further—to a new and greater growth of commerce, and advanced civilization in the New World; when the visioned El Dorado, so long sought for through spoliation, will have become an actual reality, and an innumerable population and a vast system of commerce shall be fully developed between Behring Straits and Cape Horn.

It must be conceded that strong political advantages, combined with a growing commerce, and an unparalleled enterprising people, have directed the public gaze to St. Louis as the great central city of the Republic. Her present greatness, united with her geographical position, will give her the seat of government. Free labor and the enterprise of the North, has made her wealthy, populous, and great, while slave labor and an embarrassed people has, for years, hindered the growth of New Orleans. But now that that obstruction is removed, we have only to look beyond, and consider the results of the legitimate growth of civilization in the New World. New Orleans occupies, substantially, the central position between Behring Straits and Cape Horn, with more than 3,000 miles stretching away from her on either side, north and south. Within these limits are all the climates and soils of the globe, and capable of producing all that the wants of man demand. Contemplate, in the future, these climates well populated, and these varied soils well cultivated, the whole territory of the United States actively improved for the best uses; also, the tropical regions and States of Mexico, Central and South America, made to subserve their highest uses, and the great mass of all these products seeking an interchange of markets through a vast system of railroads, almost traversing this entire land, and aided by numerous lines of improved ocean steamers, traversing its entire waters, and at least one-half of the railroads and steamers bearing their commerce to New Orleans as the nucleus and central market of the New World! Then the importance of New Orleans becomes manifest. With a mellow Southern climate, and the very gate through which untold wealth must go and come, who can tell her future? No estimates can overreach her, or speculations measure her destiny. She will be the mistress of the world, endowed with all the beauty and wealth that belong to tropical lands.

Even from this time, it will not be ten years till one-half of the grain of the Mississippi Valley will pass through her hands to distant markets. But a few years more, and well-regulated lines of fine ocean steamers will run from her wharf to Europe, Asia, Rio Janeiro, Laguira, Panama, and the Islands of the Seas.

The argument in her favor could well be detailed to an indefinite length, but the brief manner in which every subject has been herein treated, will not justify it. Those who think that climate and foundation are barriers to her future growth, do not comprehend the invincible progress of man.

Slowly man conquers the obstacles of nature that impede his progress. Even from the darkest view of the site of New Orleans, she is not so barren of natural advantages of Venice, and many other powerful cities of the Old World. However treacherous the earth may be under her feet, an enterprising, industrious, and commercial people will, in due time, overcome the disadvantages, while the vast column of water which will forever pour through the bed of the Mississippi will keep open a highway for the commercial transports of all lands. So far, the perils of sickness are not half so disastrous as they have been to the great cities of the Orient—Calcutta, Bombay, Jeddo, Pekin, and Constantinople—besides the time it is not far distant when man will master and control those terrible visitants, and drive them from his presence. No diseases have ever yet visited the South that have strewn as much desolation in their paths as did the miasmatic slavery. In its march it spread desolation, poverty, despair; but, at last, death has overtaken it, and liberty now wears her olive crown, and where slavery blighted the lands, liberty will spread green fields; where slavery mocked God, liberty will bless humanity.

The citizens of New Orleans, already coming forth from their "new birth," are casting about for a new career in commerce. In this connection, it is gratifying to quote from a recent address, by Wm. M. Burwell, Esq., of Virginia, before the Mechanics' and Agricultural Fair Association of Louisiana.

Touching the commerce of the South, Mr. Burwell has the following:

Nothing will tend more rapidly to develop the ability of the South than the encouragement of internal and foreign commerce. Much of the first is conducted by rail and telegraph, and with the extraordinary facilities of the North and West for communicating with and supplying the trade territory which would seem to belong to our merchants, it is not surprising that they should control that trade. We also must have a cheap and rapid means of transmitting intelligence and values. Southern railroads should be worked on certain general principles adopted elsewhere.

1. All railroads connecting on the same gauge should be consolidated under a single administration, and upon as long, direct lines as possible.

2. They should pro-rate tariffs and schedules, exchange burden

cars, employ depots and turn-tables in common with other roads upon the same gauges; in all terminal cities they should run the rail to the wharf, and transfer freights to and from the large shipping at the lowest charge possible.

3. They should make fast freights and through freights, and should in every manner afford every accommodation which may promote the intercourse between the merchant and planter. It is especially important that they should organize locomotive factories and mills for rolling or re-rolling rails, for the encouragement of our own industrial interests.

But the chief advantage of Southern commerce must consist in opening a trade with the countries to the south of us, in supplying those populations with our productions, and especially in conducting the trade between the great Northwest and the tropical regions. When we regard the trade between the United States and Europe, we must be impressed with the fact that, with the exception of the Southern staples, nothing is produced on this side of the Atlantic which may not be found in an equivalent latitude on the other. The Northern manufactures have to be protected by a high tariff from the competition of trans-Atlantic skill, while the provisions of Wisconsin come in direct conflict with those of Wallachia. This trade labors under the disadvantage that it must cross the ocean both ways at our expense. When, however, we regard the great market of Mexico, Southern, Central, and Insular America, and consider the growing millions of the Northwest, that consume such an immense value of tropical products, we must perceive that the commercial interests of the United States must be developed to much greater advantage upon this side of the Atlantic, because the burdens of competition will be thrown upon the trans-Atlantic merchant, manufacturer, and farmer.

There is every encouragement to believe also that much of the South Sea commerce will be conducted by steam, to avoid the trade winds, calms, and currents of those latitudes. Occupying, then, the Gulf ports; backed by deposits of iron and coal of excellent quality and unlimited extent; seated at the points where those reciprocal commodities can be best exchanged, why should not the ports of the Southern States conduct and control much of this invaluable trade? There are great obstacles to its organization, but these obstacles can be removed. They consist chiefly in foreign duties and the delays of trade. We have every reason to hope that the Federal Government can secure for us something like a reciprocity treaty, by which the cost of exchange may be reduced; or, indeed, that it may purchase for us a right of daily intercourse with all the ports around the Gulf, with no other restrictions than those between New Orleans and Galveston. The effect of daily steam to Havana and Vera

Cruz, with submarine and overland communication with interior Cuba and Mexico, upon the merchandise and produce markets of the Southern States, cannot be computed. Steamships, owned, manned, and commanded by Southern men, fitted out in Southern ports, exchanging interior against tropical products, and transmitting these products with rapidity, would bring an activity, energy, and strength to the South which would soon repair the past. To effect this desirable object, it would be necessary to invoke the aid of the Northwest; and you, Mr. President and gentlemen of the Association, could not render a better service to the South than, acting in conjunction with the authorities and Chamber of Commerce of this and other cities in the South, to open a communication with the Northwestern cities upon the subject. There are physical obstructions at the mouth of the great river which might also be called to the attention of the powerful interest alluded to.

We cannot see anything extravagant in the request of Mr. Burwell for free trade for the South with the adjacent ports of Mexico, Central and South America; and in all probability the day is not far distant when free trade will be established all over the American continent, from Cape Horn to Behring Straits.

Let us have a growing and expanded America, and "no matter in what region a desirable product is bestowed on man by a liberal Providence, or fabricated by human skill. It may clothe the hills of China with its fragrant foliage; it may glitter in the golden sands of California; it may wallow in the depths of the Arctic seas; it may ripen and whiten in the fertile plains of the sunny South; it may spring forth from the flying shuttles of Manchester in England or Manchester in America—the great world-magnet of commerce attracts it alike, and gathers it all up for the service of man."

The destiny of New Orleans is fixed, and unless the waters of the Mississippi and the Gulf dry up and the seasons change, and "the desire of man fails," she will be the greatest city in the world.

OTHER CITIES.

Besides the five great cities of which we have just spoken, others of secondary importance will take their places and share in the glory of the Republic—Philadelphia, Baltimore, Boston,

Cincinnati, Memphis, Omaha, Kansas City, Denver City, Salt Lake City, Astoria, and another great one on the Gulf of California, all of which will be great, wealthy, and powerful.

POLITICAL POWER.

But there is a political growth, too, which must keep pace with the growth of arts and agriculture. From our present number of States we shall probably grow to 57, when all the Territories are made into States, as follows: 17 belonging to the Atlantic Slope, 24 to the Valley States, and 16 to the Pacific Slope. This, too, will throw the political preponderance into the hands of the Valley States.

With all this great advance, this magical transfer of power, who can be so simple as to rest in the belief that with it will not come a change of national empire, or a removal of the Capital of the Government to the banks of the great Mississippi? Who is so foolish as to think that an ambitious, industrious, and successful people, with millions of population and millions of treasure in their favor, will not demand, in due time, the removal of the Capital from its present location to their midst? It will come, and come soon. National gravity will bring it.

In support of this conclusion, we submit the following remarks by Dr. Wm. Elder, of Washington City, who is one of the ablest statisticians in the country:

The time has come, the necessity is upon us, our security and prosperity demand the extension of the Monroe doctrine to the *commerce* of the continent. England is ready to give up empire in government for dominion in the trade of America. The only supremacy she cares for now is that of her labor. Her only fleets and forces for invasion and conquest are her mercantile vessels and her manufactures, and our defenses are not in our monitors and forts, but in our Custom Houses. Political liberty and independence are not the only care of government; industrial freedom and independence are the best security for these, and all that is most worthy of living for in this world besides. It is the prime duty of every community to provide and defend for its members all the conditions of individual prosperity which a sound policy can command.

Theories manufactured by the master commercial nations, and designed to hold their old-time colonies in industrial vassalage, must not be allowed to override universal experience. Universal, we say, for it is proved in the history of the past that no nation has risen to the rank of a first-rate power, in politics or war, in commerce or wealth, that has not studiously and persistently diversified its industries to its utmost capacity. England herself is one of the best among the examples. France and Germany are relatively as prominent; and Portugal and Turkey prove it as well, by the exhaustion they have suffered from abandoning the policy of self-protection, or self-defense against foreign invasion of their labor markets at home. As to the much vaunted Anglo-French treaty of commerce made in 1860, which free-traders are accustomed to claim as a partial advance of their doctrine, it is demonstrable that it is quite as protective of the home industry of France, and more effectively framed for that purpose, than the Morrill tariff of March, 1861, was for the United States. The authorities abroad have not given up the struggle, but they have abandoned the hope of extending their doctrine of free trade among the nations. The London *Economist* of 17th of December, 1864, concedes that its "creed is not only stationary, but retrograding," adding that "in America (meaning the United States), the Canadas, Australia, and the Anglo-Saxon colonies generally, the belief in protection seems to have acquired a new vitality. The Northern Americans have raised their tariff to figures which, but for the vast war expenditure, would almost extinguish trade; the Canadians try to meet every fresh expense by raising some duty on an import, and a parliament has just been elected in Victoria, pledged to introduce a system of general protection for colonial industry. Nothing is to be imported which can possibly be made, and manufacturers are to be encouraged to make by the imposition of excessive duties upon all European goods which compete, or may compete, with local productions."

The author, after a very candid, though incomplete, statement of the argument on which the Australian colonists rest the policy which they have adopted, concludes: "We confess we cannot quite see the immediate remedy for this state of affairs, and are inclined to believe that patience is the only remedy."

No doctrine or dogma, exposed to the test of experience, needs patience more than the one self-styled free trade, because it starts upon the false pretense of a misnomer, and never dares venture far enough from its base of supplies to win a victory in the field of trial, and hold it. Its mission of universal philanthrophy would be better described as a system of free *foreign* trade, with industry at home in hand-cuffs. It means—open the ports of the world, and the markets which they guard, to the exclusive traffic of the strongest, at the expense of destroying all the rival labor of the purchasing nation, and starving the workmen of the producing nation.

In the natural order of things, the free-traders will have to wait, as the world waited upon England, until protection had served its purpose, and would have been an absurdity and a nullity, if longer continued. Their tariff duties were in effect repealed by their supremacy in commerce, long before it was done by act of Parliament, and they must wait upon the Australian, Canadian, and other Anglo-Saxon colonists, who are still at the mercy of England's larger and cheaper capital, better organized machinery, and cheaper wages, until these struggling people have got on even ground, and are ready for a free fight for their lives.

Setting aside theories of commerce, which neither require nor tolerate any reference to history or facts, it may be asked why England, Wales, and the lowlands of Scotland, with a less area than Pennsylvania and West Virginia in the East, or Missouri alone in the West, and having neither more nor better iron and coal than either of them, and with vastly inferior food-producing power, and equally inferior command of all the supporting resources of the highest forms of industry, should nevertheless hold the commerce of the United States in their hands, make our clothing, machinery, agricultural implements, and our railroads, leaving us for our own share of mechanic labor little besides house building other than iron structures, horse-shoeing, the printing of local items, and grave digging, which of necessity must be done on the spot?

The one sole reason why England obtained the mastery of the ocean, and command of the world's business, is that she exported no raw material; and the reason why the Southern States went into ruin, by the route of rebellion, is because they exported nothing else. The trade of Germany at the beginning of the century was hides, tallow, flax, and wool, exported, for cloth and cutlery in return, and Bonaparte could make their territory his fighting ground. Since the battle of Waterloo, they have been making their own clothes and cutlery, and his nephew, with more resources and stronger alliances, was obliged to keep within the line of war with Austria, which the rest of Germany prescribed.

POPULATION.

Another most interesting feature of our subject, and the one upon which everything depends, is the future growth of population in the United States. In 1790, or about the time of the adoption of the Federal Constitution, we had a population of 3,929,827, a little more than the present population of the State of New York. Now we have grown up within the lifetime of a human being to a population of 31,443,322. But, as in other departments of our progress, we have not reached our full growth in population. Even the thought of what we can and will be is overwhelming.

In England, the density of population is about 230 persons to the square mile; but England is, in some measure, the workshop of the world, and supports, by her foreign trade, a greater population than her soil can nourish.

In France, the density of population is about 160. In Germany, it varies from 100 to 200. Assuming, on these grounds, that the number of persons whom a square mile can properly sustain, without generating the presence of a redundant population, in our rich country, is 490, the number authorized by a writer in the *Britannica Encyclopedia*. This would, when the country is fully developed, give the Atlantic Slope a population of 219,970,310, and to the Valley States a population of 761,302,530, and to the Pacific Slope a population of 483,754,460, and to the whole country a total population of 1,465,027,400, a body of people infinitely beyond the comprehension of the human mind. Even the half of this number of inhabitants would make us a greater nation than ever ruled on earth.

The estimate above gives us a population greater than the entire present population of the world. But the grandeur of the thought still swells when we consider that in a little more than a century, or beginning with a new era, our numbers will well nigh approximate this great growth.

It is estimated that, of the increase, 1,329,066 is the natural increment; the balance, 2,340,394, by emigration—the Northwest filling up with the hardy, industrial classes coming hither from Europe and the older States.

Population of the United States in 1850, 23,191,876; in 1860, 31,429,891—increase, 35.52 per cent.

The increase of the population of the Northwest during the last ten years has been 67.9 per cent., while the ratio of increase in the whole country has been 35.52. The population of the Northwest, by the census of 1860, was 28.85 per cent., nearly one-third. Of the total increase in the population of the country, 44.67 per cent. was in the Northwest alone. An increase at the same ratio during the present decade will give the Northwest in 1870 a population of 15,212,622—an increase of 6,139,567. Massachusetts, the most densely populated of all the States, has 157.8 inhabitants to the square mile. A like density of population in the Northwest would give us a population of 133,011,198. A density of population equal to that of England (230 per square mile) would give an enumeration of 279,846,120.

The popular vote of 1852 is copied from the census compendium, (1850,) p. 50; that of 1860, from the census returns. Under the old apportionment (1850), the Northwest had 24.31 per cent. of the members of the House of Representatives, or a fraction less than one-fourth. Under the census of 1860 she is entitled to 30.47 per cent., or nearly one-third. At the Presidential election of 1852, the Northwest cast 29.46 per cent. of the popular vote. In the Presidential election of 1860, she cast 36.24 per cent. of the popular vote—more than one-third. In the electoral college in 1860, the Northwest cast 23.14 per cent. of the vote for President and Vice President.

The following table shows the standing of the *loyal* States in respect to political power in 1852 and 1860:

	1852.	1860.
Popular vote for President	2,583,918	3,805,640
Electoral votes	205	....
Under the new census	......	210

In 1852, the Northwest cast 35.68 per cent. of the popular vote for President in the loyal States, and 34.63 per cent. of the electoral vote. In 1860, she cast 44.4 per cent. of the popular vote, and in 1864 had 40.63 per cent. of the votes of the loyal States in the electoral college.

A RECAPITULATION.

"If the course of human affairs be considered, it will appear that many accidents arise against which the heavens do not suffer us to provide."—MACHIAVEL.

"The revolutions of the human mind," says Lamartine, "are slow, like the eras in the life of nations." It is no ordinary work for a great nation to pass through a transition—to revolutionize the mental status of its people, to cool passions, and remove prejudices, kindled into heat and produced by destructive and unrelenting war—and, by reorganization and new legislation, set up a new order of things. It is not the work of a day, nor a year, but the work of time, and deliberate and far-reaching statesmanship. In every great movement, mistakes will delay a success or a victory, while wise counsels will accelerate them. Whatever may be the anxiety of statesmen to heal up the wounds of the rebellion, and to restore the revolted States to political equality and harmony in the Federal Union, the completion of the work is still in the distance. As we go forward to its end, "hills peep o'er hills, and Alps o'er Alps arise." Difficulties in the machinery of the government, arising out of unexpected interpretations of its law by men of diverse opinions, prolong the work of reconstruction. Nor can the work be thoroughly completed until an entire change and reorganization of the government has fully taken place and a new order established, substantially as follows:

I. The election of a new President, and his installment into office.

II. The formation of a new National Constitution, and, under it, the reorganization of the Supreme Court, and the making of such other changes as seem best for the safety and perpetuity of the Republic.

III. The removal of the National Capital to the Great West.

It is not possible, in the nature of things, that a Constitution framed in the infancy of a nation, and, by its own weakness and the error of laws enacted under it, sustaining and spreading the greatest moral deformity of the nineteenth century, is a fit fundamental law for the nation after having thrown off, by revolution, that great moral deformity. Nor can this great work of reconstruction and reorganization be done too hastily. "The evil in republics," said Carnot, the great French statesman, "is found in their instability, being hastily put together in the midst of civil commotions, enthusiasm always presiding over their establishment. *One* only has been the work of philosophy, and that is the United States." It most emphatically behooves our statesmen of to-day to make their work the work of philosophy. In short, out of this struggle, this transition, will come a new Republic—a new nation born into existence out of the fiery trials through which we are now passing. The conflict will go on until the deep foundations of the present

Republic are upturned by the immutable decree of Omnipotence, working in and through the American people. Practically, the form of government will not be changed, but from it will essentially come a new one, a perfect one, in so far as man is capable of constructing a perfect government—a government whose life-principles will be practical, living realities, and not vague and ill-defined and falsely applied principles. Those who still cling to the old Union, with its broken oaths, its fountains of slave tears and its treason-battered walls and its demagoguing friends—its blasted hopes and its dying form, in the belief that it is yet to rise, the same again in power, will be left to "weep over the tombs of their hopes and heroes." No such resurrection awaits it. It is gone forever. But, Phenix-like, the new Republic will arise out of the departing form of the old government, and with gigantic proportions and all-embracing beneficence and power, will encompass this whole land from ocean to ocean, and from polar snows to tropic sands. The majesty of this new government is yet beyond comprehensive conception.

Its constitution will not come by accretion, but will be the spontaneous creation of the people of the Republic; born out of the trials, experiences, and enlarged comprehensions, of a growing and progressive nation. Let us all anticipate it, let us labor for the recognition of the higher and broader truths, and let us all earnestly pray that the sun may soon rise to behold an empire of mind as well as of state!

The foundations for the new Republic must be laid in the HIGHER LAW—which is the unwritten law of all nations, the teachings of which guarantee to all people alike an equal right to life, liberty, and the pursuit of happiness, with "no restraint but those laws which are the same to all, and no distinction but that which a man's merit may originate." With this consummation justly won, who will not willingly say, happy, proud America, thine is the HIGHER LAW, and thine the consecrated home of LIBERTY!

THE UNION AS IT SHALL BE.

SELECTED.

On the rocks we read the story
  Of the revolutions grand,
Which, in ages past and hoary,
  Swept o'er mountain, sea, and land.
There we trace the mighty stages
  Of the world's historic time,
And we mark the buried ages
  By their monuments sublime;
And the lesson old earth teaches,
  By her grand symbolic forms,
Is that she all beauty reaches
  Through upheavals, fires, and storms.

History points, with solemn finger,
  To her records dim and old,
And, as thoughtfully we linger,
  Still the lesson there is told:
Through the struggles and the burnings,
  Through the stern and frantic strife,
Through the nation's fierce upturnings,
  Put they on a fresher life;
Then they pass to higher stages,
  Both of beauty and renown—
In the conflict of the ages,
  Greatness doth the nations crown.

Lo! we feel the wild upheaval
  Of a nation's hidden fires;
Right is battling with the Evil,
  And the smoke to Heaven aspires.
War, tumultuous and red-lighted,
  Sweepeth with sirocco blast,
And our green young land is blighted
  As the tempest whirleth past.
Not the death-throe of the nation
  Is this wild and awful hour;
'Tis its painful transformation
  To a nobler life of power.

As the fossils huge were buried
  In the massy folds of rock,
So our Saurian crime is hurried
  To its death-throe in the shock;

THE NEW REPUBLIC.

'Neath the Union's broad foundations
   Shall the monster Slavery lie,
While the coming generations
   Ponder o'er the mystery.
Through long periods of beauty,
   From its dark transition time,
In its march of power and duty,
   Shall the Union live sublime.

Nobler, freer, and more glorious
   Shall the future Union be;
O'er the despot's rod victorious,
   All the lands its strength shall see—
North and South in one dominion,
   One in freedom evermore;
O'er one land, on loving pinion,
   Shall the lordly eagle soar;
Northern lake, and Southern harbor,
   Cotton field, and prairie wide,
Seaside slope, and greenwood arbor,
   All shall boast the Union's pride.

On, through all the stormy trial,
   God shall bring us on our way;
Let us meet the stern denial,
   Let us watch and wait and pray.
Up from all this tribulation
   We shall rise a nobler land.
And in peerless exaltation,
   'Mid the nations envied stand.
Welcome storm, and fire, and peril!
   Fields elysian yet shall rise
O'er our war-worn wastes and sterile,
   Wrought by freemen's sacrifice.

FUTURE CIVILIZATION.

> "There is yet a boundless ocean
> For the soul of man to sail,
> A grand and golden mountain
> For his feeble footsteps to scale."
> —[MARY F. DAVIS.

Sweeping over our great country, and considering her natural advantages, her past, her present, and future growth, we are involuntarily turned to a higher consideration of her future civilization.

The growth of civilization, and the growth of a nation, is only an enlarged moral and intellectual growth of a man. Starting with a child, there must be suitable adaptations to each period of growth through life, up to mature manhood. That which is suited to the infant, is not suited to the boy; that which is suited to the boy, is not suited to the young man; that which is suited to the young man, is not suited to the full grown man; that which is adapted to the full grown man, is not suited to the mature man, whose mental powers reach out after the philosophical, the spiritual, and the infinite. So are the same steps in nations and in civilization.

Those who first put their feet upon Plymouth Rock, and the kindred shores of the Atlantic, sowed the seeds of a new and greater nation, and a new and higher civilization. The Atlantic Slope became the mother and the germ out of which the most enduring toil, the most ready industry, the greatest skill, the most comprehensive thought, and the most liberal government and religion ever sprung. From those inhospitable shores, arose, like magic, a race of Titans, with an empire's might. Soldiers, statesmen, scholars, husbandmen, craftsmen, artisans, and poets, sprung up into the first ranks of the world, quicker than any before had ever risen. From that nursery of the nation, that nursery of a new civilization, has gone out the spirit of progress over the continent, as the dove went out over the waters of chaos; and where the rude cabins of the forest once stood, now stand the busy cities of the new civilization, and the destitute and native children of the cabins are continually rising to the highest places in law and government. But the work is only begun, and the sequel will be far greater than the introduction.

While we give to the Atlantic Slope the great system of manufacturing and commercial industry, and to the Mississippi Valley her teeming millions of population, with their vast agricultural and stock growing districts, it is reserved for the Pacific Slope, with her great mountain system, to be the vantage ground whereon will culminate American civilization.

Man is a creature of the earth; his success or failure depends much upon the natural advantages of that portion of the earth on which he lives. What is substantially true of the animals of the *mammalia* kingdom is also true of man. Those animals, by instinct and by nature, have ever been found inhabiting such localities of the earth as were most adapted to their wants and necessities. Such is the instinctive and natural alliance of man all over the earth. Not only is there a natural adaptability of man to certain portions of the earth, to supply his wants and necessities under suitable temperatures, but he still owes a higher allegiance to mother earth. To a certain degree, he owes the strength and durability of his organism and his mental qualities to the physical formation of the earth, where his parents and grandparents were born and reared. As the geological character—whether mountainous, or barren sand, or fertile valley—so, to a great extent, are the organisms and mental endowments of the people of that locality. Earth, air, and food have much to do in making people what they are. As physical exercise works upon the muscles, so does good or bad air work upon the mind, through the organism.

People in a timbered country are, as a general thing, more dishonest than those in a prairie country. Thieving is very common with the inhabitants of timbered localities. In a prairie country there is more exposure; hence the embarrassments against theft. People in low valleys and bottom-lands are more sluggish and ungenerous and lower toned than people on uplands. People who live in high latitudes are energetic, industrious, generous, and love liberty; while the contrary characteristics belong to the inhabitants of low latitudes. People who live in mountain regions can never be enslaved; like the soaring eagle, they love liberty as they love the water they drink and the air they breathe. People who live upon the low lands and breathe a poor air are slaves to themselves, their passions, and their ignorance.

The rocks strewn upon the face of a continent by the hand of nature are the initial seeds of sturdy life. Districts of country with rugged surface and underlaid with granite are the sure birthplace of a hardy and industrious people, whose physical and mental endurance will be far greater than those born and reared in a country noted for its rich loam and scarcity of granite stratas. This science of NATALOGY might be developed much further, but we go on to its higher aspect.

It is an old and truthful saying that poets are born, and not made. There is a great deal implied in this, which is little understood; but history is too full of facts in support of this proposition to be controverted, and, in support of the highest application of this argument, we appeal to history. Turning back, we find that the highest civilization and the finest literature in the world was furnished by those people who lived where they inherited the inspiration and breathed the pure air of the Apennines, the Alps, and Caucasian Mountains, and also drank inspiration from the Ægian, the Adriatic, the Black, and the Caspian seas. If searching for the fountain of transcendent literature, go to Arabia, and inquire who was the author of the Book of Job—a work so sublime in its very language that its authorship is almost attributed to an inhabitant of the skies. If you wish to know from whence came the inspiration of the fathers of poetry, go to the clear and classic sky and pure air and sublime scenery of Greece and Italy, where their mountains unite in one view with their vast landscapes and beautiful waters; there will you find the homes of Sappho, of Homer, and Virgil—the land of Dante, of Horace, and Tintoretto. One unbroken line of inspired prophets, poets, and orators arose and fell under the cloudless skies of those oriental and classic lands, leaving on imperishable pages of literature the evidence of the certain adaptability of climate and country to genius. In further proof of this, we find in man's own organism the index to his nature, out of which his character and his genius will be unfolded. From the bones and muscles come durability and toil. Out of the muscles and blood come industry and ambition, and out of the blood and nervous system come aspiration and inspiration; and as the adaptability of climate and country is to feed these different parts of his organism, so will the people and the leaders of the country be.

Turning, then, to the Pacific Slope, we are to inquire for its natural advantages for producing a high civilization. On the very threshold of the inquiry we must go to nature and ask for what purpose did she rear those vast chains of rock-ribbed mountain monarchs of the earth, whose very tops reach away up into the blue ethereal above the storms, and over whose partition walls fountains of never-ceasing waters flow with a wild majesty that defies the imagination of man. For what purpose were those splendid parks and evergreen vales spread out with more than poet's beauty, and why those wild rivers that baffle man's control, and why that pure and often humid atmosphere, instinctive with a better life; why the great trees and the beautiful bays, and, above all, and grander than all, why, from those high rocks and imperceptible cliffs and summit hights, which have known no visitor but the soaring eagle, do such all-enchanting and all-inspiring views reach out and meet in still wilder romance the surging billows of an unconquered ocean? Why all these energies and displays of nature, if not to subserve some high use for man? There can be no other ultimate purpose for which to appropriate such a wonderful and such a beautiful combination of great natural sublimities and advantages.

"On the Pacific Slope are blended beneath the eye, and swept in at one sight, the sublime castellated masses of the Andes. Their bases are set in the emerald verdure of the plain, rising gently above the sea level; their middle flanks are clothed with the arborescent grandeur of pine and cedar forests. Naked above, and towering into the upper air, their columnar form of structure resembles an edifice designed to inclose the whole globe itself; but from this foundation, and rearing their snow-covered crests another mile into the firmament, shoot up volcanic peaks at intervals of one hundred miles, increasing the throats of the inner world of fire, and coruscated in perpetual snow beneath coronets of volcanic smoke and flame.

"The sublimest of the oceans; majestic rivers more worthy to be deified than the Ganges or Egyptian Nile; the grandest and most elevated of earth's mountains; superlative forest evergreen; an emerald verdure and exuberant fertility; a mellow and delicious atmosphere, imbued with purple tints reflected from the ocean and the mountains; a soft, vernal temperature the year round—whatsoever can be combined of massive and rugged mountains, picturesque landscape, and a verdant nature shining under the richest sunlight, a climate soft and serene—whatsoever of all these, blended and enjoyed in combination, will accomplish to give grace, elevation, and refinement to the social world, are here united to woo and develop the genius of our country and our people.

"In all these natural favors our western seaboard front is supremely more gifted than the classic shores of the Mediterranean and Asian seas, for fifty centuries the favorite theme of history, poetry, and song. The embellishments which old society and the accumulating contributions of a hundred successive generations add to nature, are not yet there, but these will come; and to us who fan the career of our great country whilst we live, the future, which posterity will possess and enjoy, is full of the radiance of true glory."

In fertility of soil, of climate, in rich minerals, and natural advantages and commercial facilities, the Pacific Slope is not surpassed by any part of the earth, and is more than inviting to all who know it, and but few that have ever seen it are contented to stay away. In mountain grandeur, majestic waterfalls, beautiful landscapes, free and pure air, and wild romance, it far transcends the Alps, the Apennines, or Ægian, and Adriatic in beauty, while its flowing fountains and its gushing waters give forth a purer inspiration than comes from Caucasian caves or Pierian springs.

Such a country, then, with such natural advantages for bringing out the higher nature of man, is destined at no distant period to become the home and the land of the highest civilization in the world. Not only will it bring forth a higher order of a chivalrous populace, with a society embellished with wealth and luxury, and highly skilled in the arts and pursuits of life, but it will bring forth greater poets, seers, sages, philosophers, and statesmen than have ever before walked upon the earth—men before whose genius and verse Plato, Homer, Dante, Shakspeare, Jesus, Swedenborg, Davis, Newton, Webster, Poe, and Parker, would bow with reverence, as the citizen does to the sage.

We rejoice in the anticipation for other people, in after times, of such a mountain growth of civilization, so far transcending all preceding advances of the human race; for it is sure to come, and in its maturity will, no doubt, ripen into a patriarchal government, yet to be.

But a few years more, and the charms will be lost from Saratoga, the White Hills, and Key West, and found amid the romantic scenery of Sierra Nevadas, and persons of wealth, who seek health, pleasure, and luxury will journey westward to the Geyser, Soda, Carson, and Steamer springs. Larger and grander will be the capacities, demands, and uses for summer resorts amid the beautiful scenery of the Pacific mountains. The genii of art, science, and literature will plant their rosy grottoes on the ocean side of the Rocky Mountains.

AMERICA.

Melodia rules thy destiny, O, land
Of coming years; O empire wise and grand!
America! and thou at last shalt be
The consecrated home of Poetry,
The fairer Greece, adorned with noblest art,
And bathed in sacred love from God's creative heart.
For thee, for thee, the wise Melodians throng
Even now, and chant in Heaven their morning song;
For thee, and for thy sons, methinks they sing;
They come, and angel songs as offerings bring.
For thee and for thy race, methinks they cry,
"Love, Wisdom, Inspiration, Liberty,
The four great angels of the coming time,
To their olympian goal, lead on thy race sublime!"
Thou art the rock-built Pharos, that above
Earth's ocean lifts the immortal flame of love.
E'en now thou shinest like a beacon star,
Leading Earth's myriads o'er the deep afar.
Thou art the lost Atlantides that lay,
To ancient thought, beyond the waves away;

> The New Jerusalem the ancient Seer
> Of Patmos saw, descending, white and clear,
> From highest Heaven; the rich and wise Cathay
> Columbus sought, faith-guided on his way.
> The Old, the New, the Future, and the Past
> Meet and embrace, complete in thee at last;
> Thou art the crowning flower of Earth and Time,
> The destined Eden of mankind.
> —[REV. T. L. HARRIS.

CONSTITUTIONAL GOVERNMENT.

"According to the judgment of all authors who have written of civil government, and the examples of all history, it is necessary to whoever would establish government, and prescribe laws for it, to presuppose all men naturally bad, and that they will show and exert that natural malignity as often as they have occasion to do it securely, for though it may possibly be concealed for some time, it is for some secret reason, which want of precedent and experience renders invisible; but time discovers it afterwards, and is, therefore, justly called the *Father of Truth*."—MACHIAVEL.

"Government is defined to be the union of physical force, established to control civil society. The person or persons who exercise this force are called the *supreme power*. This may be divided into different branches, as the *proposing*, the *deliberating*, the *decreeing*, and the *executive* power, which may be divided into the *administrative*, the *judicial*, and the *military*. These divisions are in a great measure arbitrary, and varied by the circumstances and characters of different nations. The manner in which the supreme power is organized, subdivided, and concentrated, is called the *form of government*."

So varied have been the forms of government under which mankind have lived; so short-lived have the governments been; so little good have they seemed to have rendered to the governed; so corrupt are rulers, so selfish and unstable is man, that the wisest of lawgivers and philosophers are often puzzled to know which form of government is best calculated to confer upon man the greatest good and surest safety while on the earth.

The long historic record, reaching from the present time to the remotest age, furnishes the unmistakable evidence that man thus far has been incapable of evolving any apparent permanent good for himself, and that in all ages the shock of revolution, the march of pestilence and famines, have led the "pious to doubt the favor of God."

The "philosophers of the uncertain sciences" have been incapable of organizing any government, or any system of society, that would stand the wear and tear of more than two or three centuries. But shall we despair, and count man and Providence a failure? Not so. The philosophers, the statesmen, and the people must learn to read aright the lessons of life and government as a great overruling and beneficent Providence has diffused them in and through all His works. The race of man is a thing of growth, like an individual or a plant. It has its natal life, its childhood, its youth; it *is* to have its manhood, age, and death, and the evolving, changing, and dying nations are but incidental and transient manifestations in the great life of the career of mankind upon earth. They are the incoherent actions of the child in its ascension to mature manhood, or from imperfection to perfection. Such is the working of nature's eternal principles, and such her progress, and in one sense mankind have been, in all ages, as good as they could be, and had it been possible at any period to turn every human being into a philosopher or divine, the world would not have been any better off than it was or is. Man cannot change the overruling Providence, "whose ways are past finding out."

But underlying all national life is a beneficent tendency, continually urging men and nations onward and upward.

Thus far, the advanced guard of the race has come up through the lower forms of despotic government, and are now struggling for more liberal forms of civil rule. Individual liberty, the highest right possible for man in society, or government, is now widely sought for through governmental republicanism.

In the United States, where it is universally conceded that this is the best form of existing government, the people have only attained to TRANSITIONAL REPUBLICANISM AND SENTIMENTAL FREEDOM. The late rebellion and the present transition through which the Republic is passing, is opening the way to organic liberty. "It will be born in a manger; but the kings of the earth shall bow before its simple grandeur and majesty."

This leads us, then, to speak of our own government.

It is a rare thing for truth and justice to be born twins. Often either is born in eventful times, but for want of good nursing and liberal culture, they struggle long for the ascendency.

Two political theories originating in the factional contentions of political partisans of diverse interests have become prominent in this government—one essentially governmental in its character, the other partisan and selfish. In defense of the two theories, upon which the friends of each contend the government was organized, much has been written and said. Yet the people seem to be only little more enlightened upon the true theory of our government, even with the additional experience and teachings of the rebellion, than in the earlier days of Calhoun and Webster.

The two theories may be stated thus:

I. The theory of Washington and Hamilton was, that in the organization of the colonies into a Federal government, over them was established onstitution, for the creation of which each colony delegated its sovereign rights. In evidence of the correctness of this position, I quote the following statement from one of Hamilton's great commentators:

"To form of a feebly connected Federal association, extending along the shores of a vast, wide continent, one people—an American nation; to reduce to peaceful co-operation discordant States; and to establish over them a Supreme Representative Government, founded on the power and sovereignty of that united people—capable of promoting and perpetuating their happiness; to substitute order for anarchy, had been the noble aim and great end of Hamilton's life."

The friends and defenders of this Federal theory of government exerted all their abilities to construct out of discordant and feeble colonies a republican or representative government, with sufficient power for self-defense, and sufficient legal organization to legislate for its people. Upon this Federal theory the government was built.

II. The modern Democratic theory is that the colonies did not delegate their sovereignty to a superior government made by the Constitution, but that they, as States, are in league, at will, with themselves, and at pleasure can dissolve the original contract and set up a new government.

Now, what are the facts? There never was, nor is now, nor can be, such a government as this modern self-styled Democratic party contend for.

There can be no such thing as a government by consent— a government at will, allowing the people to dissolve it at pleasure.

A government cannot exist without a legal existence, and the very moment it passes into the hands of a Constitution creating legislative power and making laws defensive and offensive, that moment it ceases to be a government by consent, but may be a representative government.

A man and woman may consent to marry, and if they do marry, they at once assume legal relations, and cannot dissolve their marriage by their own consent, and yet they helped to make the law that holds them together. This illustration is simple and easily understood, and applies precisely to the true theory of our government. The man and wife are not in league with each other with the power to dissolve their marriage relations at will, nor are the States in league with themselves with the power to dissolve their relations and set up new governments when they choose. Common sense itself would not accept such a heresy. All the interests of man are opposed to such a government, even if it were possible for such to be. It is plain, then, to be seen that this modern Democratic theory is a falsehood and a heresy, taught in the interest of secession.

Our government is a representative government, founded upon and controlled by the franchise of all its citizens, or, to be more definite, ours is a Federal government, having many of the provisions and characteristics of a representative government. State after State that is added to the Union, like the kindred limbs of the Banyan tree, turns to the mother source and takes root again, and adds strength to the parent power.

That our government, great and good as it is, still has some faults, there is but little doubt, but that they will be hastily corrected under a new Constitution, is equally certain. The difference of opinion between Hamilton and Jefferson upon the theory of our government may be stated thus: Jefferson says the people are fresh from the revolution, and their patriotism and desire for peace and prosperity is a sufficient guarantee for the security and perpetuity of the government, without much organic law. Hamilton says that is all very good as far as it goes, but there will come a time when bad men will rise up in the government and seek for power or for ruin, and that we must have a government by law—one well provided with laws for self-defense against foreign aggression, and bad men within. Jefferson says no, the people are all right. The result was that the master-spirit of the nation, as it has been in all times, was overruled by the well-meaning but easy and delusive charity of Jefferson. The consequence has been as Hamilton said; bad men have arisen, with the full intent of breaking up the Republic. During the fierce struggle of the rebellion, all loyal people saw the necessity of constitutional power for defense against treason and secession. To the new Constitution we look for the remedy.

In the future policy of the United States, it will be well to consider how far and in what manner it will be wise to annex new territory to the government.

It will be seen by the history of past ages, that governments of large territorial extent have only been held together by force of arbitrary and despotic tyrants and military power. It is well to heed this lesson of history, and be guided by wisdom and natural causes and consequences.

By a close examination of historical evidence and natural causes and effects, this truth is found underlying all national life, viz: that extended territorial annexations to governments lying under the same latitudes, east and west, do not so much endanger the safety and permanency of the nation, but that annexations under different latitudes, to any great extent, north and south, are dangerous to the safety and perpetuity of any government. People of extreme climates, north and south, cannot well live under the same uniform government. Natural differences of character, habits, and interests, will sooner or later arise, and demand separate and distinct legislation. All the great empires of antiquity bear testimony to this fact. Rome, in her best days, was great in extent, east and west. So was the great Persian empire. The lesson of history on this subject can be received with great profit; but, in this connection, we simply allude to the fact, and ask the attention of American statesmen to the necessity of heeding the truth, and legislating accordingly.

The American policy must, in the future, forever be firmly set against the annexation of any more southern territory—except Cuba, for which henceforth all national policy ought to be shaped. As remarked by John Quincy Adams, she gravitates toward our government—the sands of the Mississippi beat upon her shores—and she must be ours for the purposes of self-defense.

They are but sickly and short-sighted American statesmen who see visions of empire in the annexation of Mexico to this government; such an act would be the laying of a stumbling stone upon which to wreck the great Republic, and, upon its ruins, liberty, law, and learning go down. Let timely warning be given, and let every American statesman be thoroughly taught that ambition, jealousy, and cunning diplomacy can easily overleap the bounds of safety and justice.

While we would most earnestly oppose the annexation of territory to the United States, we would ever hold it the mission of the great Republic to extend the influence of her laws and institutions to all people.

Supplemental to these remarks, it may not be out of place to offer an additional word touching our country and her future.

I. He who, with the light of history before him, will look at our great Republic, will behold on another continent, and in a different form and age, its prototype in the Roman empire. In magnitude and majesty there exists a nearer resemblance than to any other; their legislation and internal politics have a great resemblance.

II. While it is true that the policy of conquest and annexation by any government is a dangerous policy, and sooner or later is the chief cause of a nation's decline, it is nevertheless the tendency of all governments, who have the power, to extend their dominions. It is the same selfish and avaricious spirit in a nation that works in the individual. We cannot expect the great Republic to be so unselfish as to be free from this extravagance; therefore, contemplating it as the inevitable tendency of power and profit for the Republic to seek dominion over the continent of North America, may not her statesmen heed the admonition of old, that "there is a way that seemeth right unto a man, but the end thereof is the way of death"? Colonies have always proven themselves to be the greatest source of war to any nation, and therefore ruin; next to colonial extension is annexation.

There is but one condition that could possibly be ingrafted into such a policy that would prolong the life of the Republic, and that is to extend the dominion in such a ratio as to give the preponderance of the government to the North, so as to compel Southern obedience to the laws of the land. It is a truth in all history that governments in southern countries are of shorter duration, more fickle and unstable, than northern governments. The mercurial nature of the inhabitants of warm or southern climates unfits them for good and permanent society or government. They excel in the fine arts, are light-spirited and buoyant, and indulge in sunny ease.

The lesson of history is equally instructive in teaching that northern nations occupy the most elevated rank in the scale of lofty and severe acquirements, scientific and literary; that their society and governments are more permanent; that the people themselves have a higher bearing, are more jealous of their purity and nobility, and that they reject the intermingling of blood with inferior races. For these causes the future of the Republic must be intrusted to the Northern people, even if it be necessary to extend our bounds to the Arctic circle.

III. Whatever legislation the law-making power of the Republic may deem best for its safety and permanence, they must keep in view the absolute necessity of resting the fundamental or organic law on permanent and unchangeable principles. A government must stand on first and fundamental principles as a sure guarantee of its long continuance, no matter how many revolutions it may chance to pass through. This doctrine was taught first by Aristotle, then by Machiavel; after him by Lord Brougham; after him by some of our own statesmen.

IV. Though colonies are the greatest source of war to any nation, civil wars are the most deplorable of all wars. They not only distract the internal arrangement of the country and engender local jealousies and factional strife, but a greater difficulty than all, as Mr. Calhoun thought, is, that no nation can carry on a civil war without going beyond its own laws, and by thus doing, it exposes itself to the denunciations of all the demagogues and disappointed partisans.

It is said to be the part of a wise general to prepare for a defeat as well as a victory; and every nation ought to have in reserve a code of laws to meet unforeseen difficulties, created by bad men, who, actuated by ambitious motives, but disappointed by defeat, endanger the public safety. The late rebellion furnishes a profitable lesson on this point. All loyal men remember how earnestly President Lincoln and his friends contended that the war was prosecuted according to the Constitution, while the enemies contended otherwise; while the facts are that there was no Constitution, or but little, about the whole struggle.

A *supreme necessity*, higher than all law, and controlled by *power* and a *divinity* that shapes our ends, were the primary and underlying means that saved the Republic. God be thanked for the salvation!

NO MORE WAR.

"When we consider—for the feelings of nature cannot be dismissed—the calamities of war, and the miseries it inflicts upon the human species, the thousands and tens of thousands of every age and sex who are rendered wretched by the event, surely there is something in the heart of man that calls upon him to think! Surely, there is some tender chord, tuned by the hand of its Creator, that struggles to emit in the hearing of the soul a note of sorrowing sympathy. Let it then be heard, and let men learn to feel that the true greatness of a nation is founded on the principles of humanity, and that to avoid war where her own existence is not endangered, and where the happiness of man must be wantonly sacrificed, is a higher principle of true honor than madly to engage in it."—THOMAS PAINE—*Prospects on the Rubicon.*

Everywhere in society we find evidence that civilization is elevating and beneficial to man. Step by step he conquers the elements of nature and turns them to his use. He has triumphed over the winds and the waves, and sent the fruit of his lands to the markets of distant nations. Miasmatic swamps have been changed into fertile lands, and mountains have been tunneled; storms, pestilence, and famine have almost yielded to his genius and his art. By science he has taken to pieces and explained the functions and uses of his own organism, and with one grand triumph he has mastered the relation of mind and matter. With the progress of another cycle he will control the storms, navigate the air as he does the waters, and call the rain as he willeth. Slowly but surely is the onward tendency to his complete triumph over all nature that hinders his safety, happiness, and prosperity. In view of such an ameliorating progress, may we not be safe in looking forward to no distant day, when the moral strength of nations will have become so strong that, when put in council with honor and justice, they will outweigh the passions, and ambition, and error of men, and thereby prevent any more war? Who would not gladly hail such a time, when wars shall cease to be; when no other Sesostris, Cambyses, Alexander, Tamerlane, or Napoleon, would deluge the world again with human blood? Such a time is surely coming. It will come as a result of the influence of a principle unfolding in governments.

Before the days of Sir Isaac Newton, astronomy appeared vaguely to the scientific world; but the discovery of a great law, controlling and guiding all planetary and material movements, at once revealed order and harmony everywhere in nature. Such a law in human society did Charles Fourier seek to discover, the application of which would bring peace, plenty, and happiness to every member of the human family.

May we not look further for some law or principle, the proper application of which in human government will prevent war?

The philosopher might recommend a superior endowment of moral gravity; the chemist, a principle of political affinity. Yet neither of these would suffice to overrule evil diplomacy and artful ambition. The remedy can only be found in POWER—power, containing lenity, wisdom, and justice. Power is stronger than gravity, stronger than affinity, and can easily dethrone ambition, or destroy diplomacy. What is power? In nature, it is the inherent or natural capability of a thing to subserve a certain purpose. In mechanics, it is the most formidable capacity of mechanical combination. In man or government, power is the most formidable use of will and capacity. What statesman is not ready to concede that power, under the guidance of wisdom, justice, and lenity, may not be so delegated and adjusted by the civilized nations of the earth as to outweigh human passion and human ambition, and thus prevent any more war?

Another evidence of this final triumph of man over barbarism and error is that, as we come down the stream of time, we find that the causes of war are not so trifling and foolish in their character as in olden times.

The progressive tendency of all human affairs unmistakably points to the time, not far distant, when the advanced statesmen of enlightened nations will labor for a solution of this great BARBARIAN PROBLEM. It must be solved in vindication of the law of progress, and the providential success of man's creation and career upon earth.

In support of this far-reaching proposition of our age, thousands of the most enlightened of the race have given their testimony and anticipated the final advent of a universal peace, a golden era—

> "When Peace on earth will hold her easy sway,
> And man forget his brother man to slay;
> When milder arts shall martial arts succeed,
> And both will march to gain the immortal meed."

Of the many humanitarians who have earnestly desired this great triumph of civilization, I am happy to present in support of this article the blazing eloquence of Victor Hugo, who is to-day the tallest column of intellectual and enlightened progressive humanity now in the world. He is the Humboldt of the age in moral and civil progress. He says to Europe:

A day will come when you, France—you, Russia—you, Italy—you, England—you, Germany—all of you, nations of the continent—shall, without losing your distinctive qualities and your glorious individuality, blend in a higher unity, and form a European fraternity, even as Normandy, Brittany, Burgundy, Lorraine, Alsace, all the French provinces, have blended into France. A day will come when war shall seem as absurd and impossible between Paris and London, between Petersburg and Berlin, as between Rouen and Amiens, between Boston and Philadelphia. A day will come when bullets and bombs shall be replaced by ballots, by the universal suffrages of the people, by the sacred arbitrament of a great sovereign Senate, which shall be to Europe what the Parliament is to England, what the

Diet is to Germany, what the Legislative Assembly is to France. A day will come when a cannon shall be exhibited in our museums, as an instrument of torture is now, and men shall marvel that such things could be. A day will come when shall be seen those two immense groups, the United States of America and the United States of Europe, in face of each other, extending hand to hand over the ocean, exchanging their products, their commerce, their industry, their arts, their genius—clearing the earth, colonizing deserts, and ameliorating creation, under the eye of the Creator.

And, for that day to arrive, it is not necessary that four hundred years should pass: for we live in a fast time; we live in a current of events and of ideas the most impetuous that has eve swept along the nations; and at an epoch when a year may sometimes effect the work of a century. And to you I appeal—French, English, Germans, Russians, Sclaves, Europeans, Americans—what have we to do to hasten the coming of that great day? Love one another! To love one another, in this immense work of pacification, is the best way of aiding God. For God wills that this sublime end should be accomplished. And see, for the attainment of it, what, on all sides, He is doing! See what discoveries He causes to spring from the human brain, all tending to the great end of peace! What progress! What simplifications! How does Nature, more and more, suffer herself to be vanquished by man! How does matter become, more and more, the slave of intelligence and the servant of civilization! How do the causes of war vanish with the causes of suffering! How are remote nations brought near! How is distance abridged! And how does this abridgment make men more like brothers! Thanks to railroads, Europe will soon be no larger than France was in the middle ages! Thanks to steamships, we now traverse the ocean more easily than we could the Mediterranean once! Yet a few years more, and the electric thread of concord shall encircle the globe, and unite the world!

When I consider all that Providence has done for us, and all that politicians have done against us, a melancholy consideration presents itself. We learn, from the statistics of Europe, that she now spends annually, for the maintenance of her armies, the sum of five hundred millions of dollars. If, for the last thirty-two years, this enormous sum had been expended in the interests of peace—America meanwhile aiding Europe—know you what would have happened? The face of the world would have been changed. Isthmuses would have been cut through; rivers would have been channeled; mountains tunneled. Railroads would have covered the two continents. The merchant tonnage of the world would have increased a hundred-fold.

There would be nowhere barren plains, nor moors, nor marshes. Cities would be seen where now all is still a solitude. Harbors would have been dug where shoals and rocks now threatens navigation. Asia would be raised to a state of civilization. Africa would be restored to man. Abundance would flow forth from every side, from all the veins of the earth, beneath the labor of the whole family of man; and misery would disappear! And, with misery, what would also disappear? Revolutions. Yes, the face of the world would be changed. Instead of destroying one another, men would peacefully people the waste places of the earth. Instead of making revolutions, they would establish colonies. Instead of bringing back barbarism into civilization, they would carry civilization into barbarism.

WHO IS THE TRUE VOTER?

In these radical times, when almost everybody seems intent on something new in government or religion, there are divers notions being set forth in favor of a change of the status of the right of suffrage, and imposing qualifications heretofore unknown to the laws. Some are determined on making a property qualification, others in favor of an educational qualification. It has not appeared yet that the arguments in favor of either of these changes are satisfactory or convincing.

The importance of all legislative changes affecting the relation of the citizen to the General Government or the State, depends upon two fundamental conditions, as follows:

I. The right of the State or General Government to change the relation of the citizen.

II. The necessity for a change.

When governments are founded, their laws ought not to be changed for light and trivial causes.

A civil government, whether a monarchy, a despotism, or a republic, is founded upon certain general principles declaring the character and functions of the government, and the relation it bears to the citizens; and whenever the legislative power of either form of government departs from those general principles, and begins a wholesale system of special legislation in support of ideas and dogmas generated in peculiar localities and by peculiar men, for special and local interests, that moment the government departs from its civil and national sphere, and becomes a party in the special interests of society; and from thence it becomes a party to the religion of its citizens, and finally goes to ruin.

The United States, in its organic law, declares its own character and defines the relation of the citizen to the government, and in that definition is incorporated the right of suffrage, without educational or property qualifications.

In the organization of a representative government, the people are called upon to choose their representatives, in whose trust they are to confide all their political interests. The representatives once chosen, and having met in convention, the question naturally comes up, whom do they represent? Do they represent the educated men, the school-masters, and college professors, with their educational qualifications, or do they represent the bankers, merchants, etc., etc., with their property qualifications?

Is this the kind of representative government that derives its just power from the consent of the governed? Is it the kind of government that holds those truths to be self-evident that all men are created equal? Most certainly not. In the organization of a purely representative government such as the United States is, the first thing for the convention to declare is, that all men are created equal, and, in governments or out, are entitled to life, liberty, and the pursuit of happiness. The next thing for them to declare is, that the just powers of government come from the consent of the governed. These fundamental truths admitted and declared, the question naturally arises, who are the governed? Are they only the people that have property and education? No; they are those who, by their voluntary consent, accept the government and the laws and privileges growing out of those fundamental principles, enunciated for its foundation. All people, then, living on the territory of such a government, are citizens in the fullest and freest sense of the term, whether they be hewers of wood or drawers of water, noble or ignoble. The next step to be taken is for the government to provide for its maintenance and the protection of its rights. To do this, it must call upon every citizen to contribute a portion of his money from year to year for its support. Again, for self-protection it must provide by law that its citizens are always under obligation to come, when called for, and defend the government to the extent of their lives. These provisions made, the next step is to make regulations for future legislation, or future government. To do this, the derivative power has but to turn back to the fundamental authority, the governed, and regulate the whole matter in their hands—and the work is complete.

We, therefore, see that a representative government is founded wholly upon the consent of the governed, and the governed must, by taxation, support it, and, by military service, defend it. In each case the whole people are alike bound, and should be represented. To provide the most practical way for facilitating the action of the governed in political affairs, the government selected the ballot-box, and conferred upon her citizens the privilege of the franchise. By this means the whole people, every citizen of the government, could have a voice in declaring who should govern, and, in pursuance of the inalienable rights of all, and the just powers of government being derived from the consent of the governed, representation, or the qualification to vote, was based upon citizenship, and not upon taxation, as many claim, for taxation is an implied obligation, falling upon all who place themselves or property under the protection of the laws. The privilege of the franchise was conferred upon all whom the law made citizens, and to whom the government could look for service and protection. The franchise is broader than taxation—it is as broad as liberty.

Therefore, whoever undertakes to impose, in these times, property and educational qualifications, strikes at an abridgment of the liberty of the citizens, and unites the work of the state with the work of society—a thing illegitimate and dangerous to any government.

The same reasons that demand a property qualification to-day will next year demand an aristocratic qualification.

In thus contending that the privilege of the franchise is coequal with liberty and citizenship, I do not lose sight of the necessity for enlightened, law-abiding citizens as the most valuable support and security to good government. Nor have I lost sight of the fact that nine-tenths of the elections in our great cities are carried by the mob and the rabble, and that majorities are too often obtained by demagoguing and corrupt influences. The realities of these things are sickening and saddening to the heart. It is a shame and a disgrace to any people in an enlightened nation to have their great cities, with all their wealth and commerce and government, ruled by the mob and the rabble.

But the remedy cannot be found in prescribing qualifications for those who vote, other than the years of maturity and compliance with the naturalization laws. The remedy is to be found in a different direction. No nation has ever suffered serious special and local evils from the increase of its own people; they are as the children of the same household; but all nations have been sooner or later sorely afflicted by the infusion of foreign elements, and while it is true that immigration is the underlying stimulus to progress and civilization, it is also true that no nation can long survive the fluctuations of society unless controlled and ruled by its own citizens. Trace the evidences of history, and this truth grows into grand proportions. I, therefore, unhesitatingly assert that America *must be ruled by* AMERICANS. And when I say that Americans must rule America, I mean that American ideas and principles must rule, and mold our institutions and give character to our society.

It is the foreign mob and rabble that carries our elections in many of our great cities. The remedy for this evil must be found without impairing the relation of the citizen to the ballot.

The same reasons that demand an educational qualification to-day will demand a religious one next year.

Let it go out over the land, as it now is the law, that the citizens of the United States, at all times and under all circumstances, except for the disabilities imposed for crime, shall be fully entitled to the franchise.

Let the government look after the citizen, and let society look after the individual, and the mutual interest of both, by restraining the wrong and encouraging the good, will increase wealth and stimulate the cause of education and religion.

THE LABOR QUESTION.

"There is no real wealth but the labor of man. Were the mountains of gold and the valleys of silver, the world would not be one grain of corn the richer; no one comfort would be added to the human race. In consequence of our consideration for the precious metals, one man is enabled to heap to himself luxuries at the expense of the necessaries of his neighbors, a system admirably fitted to produce all the varieties of disease and crime, which never fail to characterize the two extremes of opulence and penury."—SHELLEY.

The growth of society is continually unfolding vexed questions for time and experience to solve. One of the greatest is that of labor, or how shall each individual human being, by his own best use of himself or herself, provide most bread and raiment, to shelter from hunger and storms. This is one of the great questions of the world. It never has been solved, it never can be. All that can be done by advanced wisdom and experience is to correct errors and conform to the best rules of economy and compensation.

The old idea wrought out of the labor question years ago by the moral reformers of Europe was, that as civilization advanced, the prospects and comforts of the great mass of mankind darken and decline. This conviction presented to the well-wishers of the race an unsolvable problem, growing out of the great army of laborers that were yearly increasing in the over-populous regions of European civilization. But a new reckoning taught that such a result sprung from a false civilization, and not from a true and just organization of society.

In America, the labor question does not present itself as it does in Europe. There they deal with it collectively, here individually. In fact, our country is too new to demand any considerable discussion in detail upon this question. Even in our growing cities, those who find the demand greater than the supply can easily make their way to fertile lands, which they can claim as their own.

The recent agitation of the eight-hour question throughout the country is a ridiculous farce, played at the expense of the ignorance and blindness of those who are the actors.

Let us look at this for a moment. There are two wide paths in life to travel; one is the path of industry, the other the path of idleness. The path of industry leads upward, the path of idleness leads downward, and whoever does not travel one will travel the other. There are depots, stations, and resting places on all roads. These give pleasure to the traveler. Now, any man who undertakes to travel on both roads at the same time, soon becomes wayward.

Physiologists will tell us that at best eight hours for sleep is sufficient for the demand of any human organism; that in this length of time the whole system can recuperate its lost vitality. Now, suppose that of the twenty-four hours, eight be devoted to sleep and eight to labor, what will the other eight be devoted to? In nine cases out of ten, to idleness and profligacy, for the time must be on one road or the other. But again, man's physical strength will endure more than eight hours' work, and the poor man's family demands more than eight hours' pay, therefore it is wrong to establish a system of labor the workings of which are positively injurious to society. That regulation of labor is the best which gives full employment and full compensation; any other system than this is wrong, and deserves the condemnation of intelligent people.

But there is a direction in which mechanics and laboring men can look for correction; it is in the matter of rents. Each city ought to provide through its capitalists suitable houses and low rents, corresponding to the wages of the laborers. This can be done in every city in such a way as to yield a profit to the capitalist for his investment, and make just provisions for the mechanic and laborer. It is a matter that ought not to be neglected in any of the great cities.

Touching the question of the world's labor, we present the following suggestive remarks. Who the author is we know not, but a reading of the statements cannot fail to awaken reflection and excite inquiry upon the subject of the ability of the human race, and cause many to marvel and ask again, how do so many get bread?

THE AGGREGATE LABOR OF MANKIND.—Along with the compassion that is excited by listening to a tale of want, there is apt to arise a feeling of astonishment that such a thing should be in a land like this. Perhaps, however, the true wonder is that want is not universal. One-half of the race die before they have contributed an iota to the world's sustenance or their own.

One-half of those who survive the period of childhood are women, who do not, as a general thing, contribute to the production of wealth. Of the men, many are sick, many old, many are lazy, many are idle, many are wasteful, many are parasites. Those who do work, and live to the age of three-score years and ten, spend one-third of their lives in bed, one-twentieth at the table, one-sixth in recreation. Much of their time is wasted in mistakes, much of what they do succeed in producing is swept away by fire and flood. During half the year nature sleeps. One harvest in five produces a failure. Only a fraction of the earth's surface is capable of cultivation. A large part of the general labor is absorbed in the production of luxuries, in repairing the damages of war, in preparing the future for conflicts, in the transportation of produce, and in journeys. Probably not more than one-tenth of the whole amount of human force is expended in earning the world's daily bread.

The standing marvel, therefore, of society, is not that any should suffer want, but that there should be any who do not.

Every agitation of the labor question which tends to lessen the hours of toil, which man's healthy and physical system will endure, is a curse to society and the laboring population. The question has never been, nor never can be, how to lessen the aggregate of labor and prevent a superabundance, but how can society be so organized as to give employment to all willing hands, and thus enable them to provide bread and raiment for them and theirs?

It must be evident to every sensible man that the eight-hour movement is in direct antagonism to this essential object, which was set on foot by no summer patriots, who have scarcely an idea in their heads, but by the most matured and advanced thinkers in the world.

Let legislators and pretended rie s of the poor take thought and henceforth strive for an organization of society that will rear every child, male and female, honest, industrious, and healthy, with fit accomplishments for some useful avocation in life, and then certainly give him or her a place to labor, with just compensation. This end gained, an infinite good will come to all; this lost, and society will ever heave with convulsions and agitations, and the poor continue to ask for bread. It was wisely said by Malthus, the great father of political economy, that the greatest species of knowledge was that which taught a man what to do, and akin to that was that which taught him how to do it. Let the masses be taught the practical meaning and application of this truth, and labor and capital will soon find harmonious relations.

Fraternal relations must exist between labor and capital, and between labor and society. Labor must be respected and made honorable. This done, broad acres will not much longer lie idle, but be converted into fruitful and happy homes, and the shops of the cities be filled with more and better mechanics. Let all struggle to attain these results, and the happy consequences will bring a just reward.

THE FUTURE OF THE NEGRO RACE IN AMERICA.

In truth, there is scarcely an event, or a course of positive procedure, that occurs in a nation, or among people, that can be traced, in society or government, in all their effects, to that extent that will enable man to set bounds to the good or evil produced by such agencies. Nor can the wisest of men look into the future and tell what good or evil will finally work out in the path of events in the destiny of things. There is an overawing hope, however, that teaches us that all things work out good in the end. However consoling this may be to many, it is not always true.

The introduction of the negro on American soil, and the establishment of a system of slavery—the most barbarous and inhuman ever known to man, and in direct opposition to the moral and enlightened convictions of advanced mankind—was a great anomaly to human experience, and has proven a wonderful providential adjunct to the American nation.

In the language of Victor Hugo, the system of slavery in the United States was the greatest moral deformity of the nineteenth century. But shall we say, with the great Hegel, that slavery is the bridge from barbarism to civilization, and therefore a possible element to all people? Shall we confess it? If so, only in the past, for what remains of slavery in the world now lingers on the verge of ruin.

To the American people, slavery has furnished a large and bitter experience, and now that slavery is gone and the negroes remain, we are still struggling for a solution of their social and civil condition among us. The conviction of enlightened humanity admits them to equal citizenship and equal rights with the white man in the Republic. The less enlightened and strongly prejudiced deny those favors. But, however great the experience dearly bought, and regardless of whether the universal conviction could be for or against their equal rights and equal citizenship in the country, their condition and destiny is still unsettled on our continent.

They are a people to whom God and nature has given a distinctive type and special individuality, and these inherent conditions are stronger than all just forms of society or government, and will, in due time, regardless of which is the superior race, they or the white, seek independent and separate nationality and society.

Admitting the doctrine of superiority and inferiority among the races of men, there has been no inferior race which has exhibited as fine qualities of domestic and social society as the American negro has. In olden times, it was the law of mankind for the superior races to overrun the inferior ones by war or amalgamation; but a new commandment is given, and the influence of civilization and the enlightened conviction of humanity intervenes on the side of the weak, and rescues them from barbarous and uncivilized treatment. The effort to solve the great problem of their equality under the law and in society, under the same government, on this land, will continue for a while, until the negroes, as a people, grow to a just conception of liberty, society, and government, and then the condition will ripen among themselves and ourselves to contrive and develop for them a separate home and government. They will demand it, our people will aid it; and, this consummated, the problem will be solved, and not until then.

Their type and individuality, shielded by enlightened civilization, cannot be destroyed by a war of races nor by amalgamation. Therefore, possessing the nature and qualities they do for obedience in society and devotion to government, they are destined to become a great people on the western hemisphere, with good government and social society, embellished with all the refinement of advanced civilized life, with a well regulated industry and a rich commerce.

What part of the hemisphere will be allotted to them—whether a part of the United States, a part of Mexico, or of Central or South America—is yet to be determined. This much, however, is certain: that they will remain somewhere on the hemisphere, and adjacent to the tropics.

It would be a wise provision of our government to set apart Texas for those people, and begin the work of organizing a colonial government, and encourage their emigration to it. Not compel any by force to go, but provide well for their security, their government, and their homes, and the great majority will soon accept the offer. It is impossible to devise any scheme that would secure the *immediate* separation of the negroes from the Anglo-Saxons, and give them an independent government. They are too numerous, and the work would be too great to accomplish in a year or even a generation. Besides, an immediate removal would be a greater calamity to the South, viewed from a pro-slavery stand-point, than was their freedom without compensation or their elevation to suffrage. Their labor is an absolute necessity, and cannot be dispensed with for years to come. The new government for them is a thing of the future, but WILL COME, and its foundations ought to be laid soon, and will be, if our Government acts wisely in view of the great future.

May God speed the day when the problem will be solved and peace be restored to the Republic, and embittered feeling among the people be forgotten, and the two races stand independent, but as friends, each sharing alike liberty and civilization, and actuated by the highest motives known to mankind.

TO THE YOUNG MEN OF THE REPUBLIC.

"Each man is capable of rendering high service to humanity; but whether humanity gets it from him, or the reverse, will ever remain for the world to decide."—A. J. DAVIS.

"There is a noble manhood that can mingle in every action of daily life and never be defiled; a guard which God doth place around the faithful, that is stronger than steel and brighter than gold."—LINTON.

Taking this opportunity for recording a word that may chance to meet the eye of some whom I shall never see, I desire, as one who has had much bitter experience thus far in life, to impress with profoundest conviction on every youthful mind, both male and female, that the grandest thing that each of you can attain to is INDIVIDUALITY — that is, to be YOURSELF, and not try to be anybody else. You may regard this simple and easily attained, but no matter, attain it. To be yourself, really and truly, is greater than to try to be Alexander or Semiramis. Individuality will impress you with the nobleness of your existence and the sublime mission of life. Take your own chance in the world and depend upon yourself for success.

You will be sorely tried many times by the adversities of life, but be not discouraged. Be industrious, be honest, and seek to be intelligent, and all things will work out good in the end. Let not poverty, nor sorrow, nor surrounding death, bring discouragement; for that which is best for the soul's growth, and richest of all else, is born out of sorrow and bitter experience. We behold through the tears of the storm the beautiful bow bending over the skies. Jesus had to wear the thorns before He could wear the crown; He had to pass Gethsemane before He could reach the Mount of Transfiguration. Such has been the experience of the great majority of those who have made themselves valuable to their fellows. They have come up through trials and tribulations of the most bitter kind, and for every such experience they have been enabled to render valuable service to the race. Then be not discouraged, even in the lowest walks of life, but look up; and remember that there is no excellence without great labor.

I have but little faith in the great majority of local society organizations. They are patronizing and winning, but destroy individuality. To be a citizen, really and truly, is grander than all else. I have always derived more pleasure, and, to a great extent, more profit from my books than from living friends and surroundings. Yet I do not deprecate the aid and companionship of friends. A true friend is far above price, and is twin to a true lover. Good books are unselfish and impartial; they are always companionable alike, whether in the palace or in the cabin. I continue by submitting a word of invaluable advice by the Hon. Horace Greeley, given at the close of one of his letters, touching a little discussion on a matter between him and Senator Seward. He says:

"A single word of improvement to the young and ardent politicians who may read my letter and this comment. The moral I would inculcate is a trite one, but none the less important. It is summed up in the Scriptural injunction, 'Put not your trust in princes.' Men, even the best, are frail and mutable, while principle is sure and eternal. Be no man's man, but Truth and your country's. You will be sorely tempted at times to take this or that great man for your oracle and guide; it is easy and tempting to lean, to follow, and to trust; but it is safer and wiser to look ever through your own eyes—to tread your own path—to trust implicitly in God alone. The atmosphere is a little warmer inside some great man's castle, but the free air of heaven is ever so much purer and more bracing."

You are citizens of a great Republic, which is moving to a grander destiny; be ye worthy of elevated citizenship; be honest; be temperate and industrious; cultivate love of home and country; believe in God. I have a firm conviction of the existence of a great overruling principle of Wisdom, Love, and Law.

NATIONALISM, OR PATRIOTISM.

"One theme of duty still remains, and I have placed it alone, on account of its peculiar dignity, sacredness, and importance." The largest and grandest definition of filial love is said by some writers to be a love of country—loyalty, patriotism. The necessity of this devotional sentiment or principle, by the citizen to the government, is just as important as the devotion of the individual to society.

In all ages of the world, patriotism has given to the citizen the qualities of the hero, and furnished the orator, the statesman, and the poet with themes of unequaled magnitude and grandeur. It was said that, in an older day, to be a Roman citizen was greater than to be a king; and in the face of that Arabian declaration that all that a man hath will he give for his life, the Greeks of yore, imbued with an undying patriotism, would rather suffer death, even by their own hands, than become aliens to their native land. Patriotism is yet a source of living inspiration to the human race, in every form of society and government, and no nation ought to neglect its cultivation.

It was an inborn patriotism that warmed the heart of the great Hungarian chief, Kossuth, and made him say in monotone, in answer to a solicitation to go and bring his friends and live in this country, "But this is not our native land."

He who writes of his country must in some form write of the patriotism of her citizens; and no man should be so forgetful as to write of his country without special regard for her patriotism, for no public sentiment is half so valuable to a government as that of deep-toned love of country.

The revolution of '76 sowed in the hearts of the American people the seeds of an imperishable devotion to the Union of these States—a devotion which nought but the foulest hand, moved by the most corrupt heart, would dare to reach forth to destroy; and though we are now in the midst of a transition, such as comes in the life of nations, when the event and the struggle vastly overawes the individual comprehension and convictions, and thus leads for a time to an unhappy condition and dire results, it needs no prophetic eye to see beyond to the new unfoldment, when union and patriotism will again walk together all over this broad land, as Enoch walked with God. But such a result will not be the fruit of a miracle; it will only come as the result of earnest and devoted toil, thus cultivating in the hearts of the American people a deep and fervent attachment to the Union.

Let it, then, go out over the land, as the united sentiment of the loyal people, that it is the duty of the American statesman to teach, as it is the law to prescribe, an unfailing devotion to the Republic. We must have a better patriotism—a patriotism founded upon a moral and intellectual growth of all the citizens of the government. This is a necessity that cannot be urged too strong. It must be evident that in times past the cultivation of patriotism has been neglected, and the bitter results have followed. This must not longer be; the battle-fields of the revolution and the great rebellion all admonish the millions that now are, and are yet to be, of the great importance of cultivated love of country. Not only must there be cultivated a wide and lasting patriotism among the masses, but there must be an elevated statesmanship. It is universally conceded that demagoguism is in the ascendency among our public men, and that the Republic has far more politicians than statesmen. Against this evil there must be a moral and intellectual public sentiment arrayed. The safety and perpetuity of the Republic depends vastly upon the moral strength and high-toned patriotism of her lawgivers and rulers, and let it be earnestly taught, in all truth, that he who is not a transcendent embodiment of moral, intellectual, and heroic grandeur, is not a worthy representative of the American people.

"There is a noble manhood that can mingle in every action of daily life and never be defiled; a guard which God doth place around the faithful, that is stronger than steel and brighter than gold."

If the Republic reaches that growth of national grandeur which has so often been vividly seen and described by illuminated minds of our and other lands, it must be reached through the self-devotion and moral strength of her citizens. Let the word go out over the land, from the highest to the lowest, that with united hands the American statesmen and the American people have struck for a higher destiny, and when some future Plutarch weighs the men of this Republic, they will be recorded as the grandest growth of the human race.

OUR SOCIAL DESTINY.

From the title of this pamphlet, it is not deemed out of place to submit a few remarks upon the future of society and the happiness of man, a subject which the wisest of men have sought to comprehend.

Starting with the self-evident truth that no infallible remedy whereby to make earth a heaven, by removing all the "ills that flesh is heir to," has yet been discovered by any mortal reformer, lawgiver, priest, or prophet, but that poverty still stalks abroad, ignorance still depraves, vice still brutalizes, and crime still entails its miseries, there is work yet to do, rules yet to prescribe, wants to satisfy, and wisdom to supply, and "he that does it to the least one of these does it also to me."

The great question of this age, and all ages to come, is what can best be done to augment human happiness, and what struggles—social, civil, commercial, industrial, and religious—has man yet to pass through before he reaches a point beyond want and envy?

It is wisely said and universally conceded by enlightened minds that man stands at the head of all organic life on earth, and is the master-work of God; that he has come up from all forms beneath, and that in his own organism may be traced and mapped out, in an ascending scale, his own career and progress upon the earth; that his first efforts were indicated and controlled by the basalar portion of his brain, which, in the earlier ages, allied him to the lower animals; that through his long experience, from the past to the present, he has been making his way from the basalar up through the domestic, the selfish, the acquisitive, and semi-intellectual functions of his mind, and that each era and age of his career has been marked by the action and control of these respective functions of his brain, and that he is now on the way up to the highly intellectual and religious development of his nature; that in coming up through the long and thorny path of the past, here and there a great mind has pointed out, in hopeful anticipation, the legitimate use and establishment of this or that form of government, or religion, or society, which ere long, and in its own good time,

Providence would call into practical existence, to subserve a better and higher use for man.

Thus, from the lowest form of despotism has the race struggled up to the establishment of "TRANSITIONAL REPUBLICANISM," and from the lowest form of idol worship has man come up to an aspiration and conception of Him who sitteth on the high and holy place. But the goal is not yet reached. The golden age is still in the distance; and though we boast of our civilization, the wisdom of our lawgivers, the knowledge of our philosophers, and the transcendent worth of our arts and sciences, our Christianity and our humanity, we can well exclaim with Voltaire—

"How dense a night still veils all nature's face."

Our philosophers and men of civilization may well join in saying, with Barthelemy: "These libraries, pretended treasuries of sublime knowledge, are but humiliating depositories of contradictions and errors." And may we not say, with Charles Fourier, the master social spirit of the world: "Alas! it is too true. During the twenty-five centuries that the moral and political sciences have existed, they have accomplished nothing for the good of humanity. They have served but to increase human perversity, and that in proportion to the improvement of their reformatory theories; they have succeeded only in perpetuating poverty and crime, and in constantly reproducing different scourges under different forms. After so many fruitless trials for the amelioration of society, there remains to the philosophers nothing but mortification and despair. The problem of human happiness is an insuperable obstacle to them; and is not the mere spectacle of the poor who crowd our cities enough to prove to them that their floods of philosophic light are but floods of darkness?"

There is great force in these remarks of Fourier, but he overlooks the growth of the race of man, in conformity to an eternal code of immutable laws, enacted by an overruling Providence, which brings perfection out of imperfection, and order out of disorder, and finally makes ripe the fruit on the tree of all life.

We quote again from this great man: "Meanwhile, a universal

disquietude attests that mankind has not yet attained to the destiny to which Nature would lead it, and this disquietude seems to presage some great event which is to change the condition of the race. The nations of the earth, harassed by misfortune, grasp eagerly at every political or religious reverie which offers them a glimmering of happiness; they are like the poor invalid who counts upon a miraculous cure. It seems as if nature whispered into the ear of the human race that it is destined to a happiness, the paths to which have hitherto been unknown, and that some wonderful discovery is about to dispel the darkness of civilization. Human reason, whatever boast it may make of its achievements, will have accomplished nothing for the happiness of man till it have procured for him that *social fortune* which is the object of all our aspirations; and I mean by social fortune a graduated wealth which places the least opulent beyond the reach of want, and insures to them in any event, as a minimum, that condition which we call a *moderate competence.*"

In this quotation we have the conception of a great mind, who in one broad glance, and with a heart of humanity, dares to look truth and the existing condition of mankind in the face, in spite of pretended infallible remedies for the sufferings of the race.

Shall we not dare to look back over the long line of history, and gather what lessons are scattered along its rugged pathway, and apply them to the great uses of the present and the future? All man's past experience furnishes profitable lessons for his present and future use. The rise and fall of empires, the decay of society, the march of pestilence, the ravages of famine, the desolation of wars, the development of ideas — social, moral, political, and scientific—all come to us from the buried past like the voice of prophecy, teaching us how to profit by the failures and successes of those who have gone before.

Though our country be young and giant in its growth, and prosperity seems to favor all her citizens, yet it is but mockery and short-sighted vanity to console ourselves with the belief of a perpetual career of peaceful and fruitful experience. Not so; our Republic has yet to pass through substantially all the bitter experiences of European and Asiatic nations. The character and results of those experiences will be somewhat different, but will be labor-pains and purifying trials, preceding each step to a higher national and individual life. History is always repeating itself in the cycle of succeeding ages; yet the race of man on earth is ever advancing up the golden way of the future, and carving for itself a grander destiny. The progress of each century shortens the distance to that golden age which has been seen in the future by illuminated minds of all times. But the question of all times is still before us, viz: "HOW SHALL WE IMPROVE MANKIND AND HARMONIZE SOCIETY?" This is the greatest question of the age. It demands the profoundest consideration of the greatest statesmen; it is before the ministers of every pulpit; it calls upon all reformers to aid in its solution. Nor can it be solved by the formation of any local and isolated societies, for "surely we have enough of abortive and imperfect efforts to reform the world! Witness the Mormon plan, the Shaker plan; the Christian, the temperance, the benevolent, and the prison reform societies; also sentimental communities, industrial communities, Odd Fellows, Freemasons, anti-capital-punishment and anti-slavery societies. These prove the efforts and love of mankind for man; but they are all local, despotic to some extent, and sadly adapted to the demands of universal justice."

It must be kept in view that the foundation for the great reform of man in state and society, must be laid in a broad and comprehensive system of education—an education that reaches every child of the State, and thoroughly fits it for practical usefulness, and makes it an ornament to society—for has there been in any other age so great a demand for mental power as in this?

With a universal system of more practical and thorough education, must be cultivated and diffused a deep ORGANIC LIBERTY through the broad extent of the whole land, a truer and a better liberty than we now have. Now it is only sentimental, not organic.

Following a deeper and broader education and liberty, must come a reorganization of society and labor. The whole process of civilization will continue to be a failure, and render the condition of the race of man more wretched, as long as the present system of society and regulation of labor is dominant. The whole present tendency is to enrich and elevate the few at the expense of the many. Aged nations become a loathsome burden to civilization because of the chronic disorders of society, engendered by a false regulation of the social fabric. Enlightened minds must hasten to evolve from the present condition of things a system of society and labor that will establish such an equality among the human species as is found among the birds and lower animals of the same species. This end must be gained as the normal condition of man.

With these desired objects gained, a true and universal education, an organic liberty, and a new organization of society and labor, the people will be fully prepared to battle for the great future. "It is something to us that our country is already the battle-field of truth and error; that here, on American soil, the problems of the world are to be solved." Then, in the solution of these problems, what will be the social destiny of man? His career upon earth is yet to be marked by great changes. Touching the destiny of our own people, there are two sources of underlying influences that are already operating in our civil, social, and religious structure: first, the natural elements and influences that belong to our own land, and which make us essentially an American people; second, the influences that are brought among us by means of emigrants from other lands. The peculiarities of foreign nations are brought here by the people that come, and germinate and crop out in the various struggles and conflicts of our society, and give us much trouble. These will eventually be overcome by the ascendency of the outwrought influences and conditions of our own land. In the ascendency of our native conditions, the American people will become more individualized and perfected, to that extent as to almost appear as a new race upon the continent. Human beauty will attain to a higher point than ever before, and the American woman will be famed as the most exalted and beautiful in the world.

We are yet to pass through social agitations and movements—commercial and free-trade agitations, labor agitations, financial difficulties, etc.—until we reach, not far in the distance, a great religious struggle, perhaps greater than mankind has yet experienced. Beyond this still will be a change of government—a melting away of materialistic and constitutional forms of government, and a blending of church and state, not such church and state as we now have, but a full growth and unfoldment of man's moral, intellectual, and executive nature, which will unfold a new social order, and unite and govern mankind under a kind of patriarchal system of united society and government. This form of government will control the race of man in his highest advances on the planet.

Let us all take courage, then, in the hope of a steady advance of civilization, and a full conviction that good will finally overcome evil on this side the grave.

Let none forget that *to be right they must do right*; and when all are fully imbued with this truth, and actuated by one all-pervading idea of the brotherhood of the race and good-will to men, then will be a true realization of what prophecy and inspiration have seen from all ages as the consummation and destiny of man on earth.

Let us, each and all, do our duty in our day and time, that we may make ourselves and the great Republic grander and better. And when some future Humboldt weighs the institutions of this age, may ours of the New Republic stand first in character, as they are first in rank, in the journey of the race around the earth!

ALASKA.

Since the first writing of this pamphlet, our Government made a purchase of the Russian possessions on the North American continent, which is now a part of our country, under the old name of Alaska.

Alaska has a superficial area of 450,000 square miles, which is more than twice as large as France. It contains a population of 54,000, which is not one inhabitant to every eight square miles. It is a cold country, and noted for its furs and fisheries. Any person who wishes to know all about Alaska is referred to the reading of Senator Sumner's great speech in favor of the purchase. It contains all about it.

RECONSTRUCTION.

"I see no path of ambition open in a bloody struggle for triumph over my own countrymen. There is no path for ambition for me in a divided country, after having so long served a united country."—STEPHEN A. DOUGLAS.

It is a great truth, taught in all history, that great national questions are far more easily disposed of by arms than by legislation, and that principles won by arms narrowly escape being lost by succeeding legislation.

In a republican government, national crimes and disorganizations are more difficult to punish and restore, than in a government whose power is concentrated in the hands of a few persons.

There are three propositions involved in the present work of reconstruction:

I. The restoration of the revolted States to constitutional and loyal relations in the Union.

II. The action of the General Government toward the freedmen.

III. The action of the General Government toward the rebels.

The course to be pursued in the whole matter lies in the path of loyalty, which is safety, and in the path of simple justice, which gives strength. Loyalty is the only means by which a republican government can save itself from a malignant enemy at home. Then, to restore the revolted States to their proper places in the Union, their control must be put in the hands of loyal men. This done, and no difficulty lies in the way of reconstruction.

"Without the help of the negro," said President Lincoln, "the Union must perish." *Universal liberty was the latent power that conquered the rebellion, and universal suffrage must be the legal power with which to reconstruct and save from destruction a broken Union.* This doctrine must be to Congress the pillar of fire and the cloud by which to guide them.

Slavery is gone forever. Attorney General Bates decided negroes to be citizens of the Government, and the recognition of the truth of that decision has since been ingrafted into the nation's life, and reconstruction can never be successful and permanent without the continued recognition of that truth. "This," said President Lincoln, "is not a government of vengeance. Then let us go forward, with malice to none, but with charity to all, and heal up the wounds, and forgive those who despitefully use us."

It must be conceded that a wide-spread system of slavery, like that in the United States, was a vast source of moral and political corruption and human debasement, and that thousands of honest and good people were led astray into the ranks of malignity and treason, who now ought to be forgiven, and no longer regarded as enemies to the Constitution and the Government. Even the worst of rebels ought to be pardoned after a short term of years, and admitted to full citizenship, except a disability against holding civil office. The North has already done good to those that despitefully used her; let her stretch out her hands in charity again.

John Brown said in his remarks, in answer to the question why sentence of death should not be passed upon him, that he was guided in his course by the golden rule, and that he believed that to interfere as he had done, and as he always freely admitted that he had done in behalf of the despised poor, was no wrong, but right. For acting upon this conscientious conviction his life was taken.

That was the treatment of the South to the North.

But when General Lee, for an infinitely greater crime, stated before a Congressional committee that he had always been taught the doctrine of State Rights, and believed that he owed a greater allegiance to the State of Virginia than to the Federal Government, and that it was for Virginia that he fought, and believed it no wrong to do so, this was "accounted unto him for righteousness," and his life was spared.

This was the treatment of the North to the South.

To recapitulate, the basis of reconstruction must be loyalty and universal suffrage; the terms, future pardon to the leaders of the rebellion. This will displace from power the enemies of liberty and secure a fraternal peace and a lasting Union. For Congress to pursue any other course than this would be to fritter away the triumphs of our arms and our institutions.

May God speed the day when the work shall be complete, and the whole nation be baptized in the new liberty, and redeemed by the HIGHER LAW!

Note.—At present, reconstruction can only be temporary, for out of this struggle will come a new Republic, born out of a new Constitution, with all-embracing provisions, that will revivify the States and cement them in stronger bonds of union than ever before, and dedicate them to higher principles of humanity, and to a loftier destiny among the nations of the earth.

WOMAN SUFFRAGE.

Among the reformatory agitations in America, the subject of woman suffrage has become prominent. But how much truth underlies the agitation, and how much good can come to the State or nation by admitting woman to the privilege of the franchise, is yet beyond comprehension. Mankind has not yet had any matured experience to prove that the equal, or preponderating participation of woman in the political control and management of States and nations, would answer the demands of well established and permanent government.

Thus far in the history of the race, woman's official position, as the ruler of a nation, has only been nominal. She has never yet made or controlled revolutions, nor carved empires and states out of chaos and disorder. She has never led the way to discovery, to colonization, nor to dominion in any of the great fields of human triumph, and whether such an unexampled political stride as to admit her to the equal use of the ballot, and equal, in the convention and the legislative halls, with men, would be conducive to the best interests of the nation, is a matter that experience alone can determine.

It is hardly possible that any statesman or jurist, however learned, can give unquestionable reasoning in favor of the justness of the principles of the Salic laws, and yet it is probable that in the repetition of history, and the perversion of human conduct, that the days of Heliogabalus and his debased Senate may find a parallel in some future legislative assemblies. Intrinsically considered, government is masculine and society feminine, and the conjoint action of the male and female, or positive and negative principle, in all forms of government, works the highest productive good.

Considering the uncertainty of the proper adjustment of these two principles—the male and female—in government, and the fatal consequences following a mistake, the acceptance of woman suffrage must be regarded as an extraordinary remedy, and one that will either kill or cure wherever administered.

The progress and enlightenment of the age seems to favor the movement as one calculated, when fully tested, to elevate and refine both society and state.

It is not intended here to discuss the subject, but simply to mention it as one of the growing agitations relating to the social and national interest of the country.

THE PACIFIC RAILWAYS.

Since the Republican party came into power, the Republic has advanced in civil and mental liberty, enlarged public policies, great measures, and newly formed States, with a rapidity unknown before in its history.

The anti-slavery sentiment of the North has triumphed over a cruel and persistent slave interest, and the nation to-day is free.

The land policy of the Republican party, with Hon. Galusha A. Grow, of Pennsylvania, as its champion, is now the wise and beneficent policy of the nation. The great measure set on foot by a few far-seeing statesmen of constructing great railways across the continent to the Pacific shore, has become a real measure of the Government, and the work far advanced. So rapid has been the progress that these great thoroughfares already penetrate the home of the Indian and the buffalo.

In 1862, Congress passed the first bill for the construction of railways and telegraphs to the Pacific. In 1865 and 1866, additional acts were passed in aid of the work. In those acts, it was provided for the construction of two great railways—one to start from Omaha, and be called the Union Pacific Railway, the other to start from Kansas City, and be called the Central Pacific Railway. Two other roads have also been spoken of, one still further north, and lying in the latitude of St. Paul, the other in the extreme south of the country, and designed for communication between New Orleans and the Pacific. The rebellion and its embarrassments narrowed the action of Congress to the construction of only two roads.

There are two prominent features connected with the two roads under construction, one relating to the routes they are to take across the continent, and the character of the country over which they pass, and the other the great commercial and civilizing purposes which they will subserve when completed.

Of the Omaha route, it is well understood that it is to cross the mountains by way of the South Pass; and to give the reader a full description of this pass, we quote from Colonel William Gilpin, who has no doubt given the facts as real as any other man; and let it here be stated that there is no formation of the continent so remarkable as that of the South Pass. It really seems as if Providence had prepared it to serve some great use for man. Colonel Gilpin says:

"To delineate the features of the South Pass, so that the topography of the plain, the prodigious Sierras which surround it, the rivers radiating out of it, and the gorges by which they commence their gentle declinations to the seas, is not easy to be done. The plain is elevated 7,500 feet above the sea. It is beyond, or west of the Cordillera. Its surface of clay is so absolutely smooth as to admit of uninterrupted vision, as over water. It is in shape a triangle, having very acute angles at the northern and southern points, and one very obtuse at the source of the Sweetwater, which is the eastern point. The western side, two hundred miles in length, corresponds with the bed of the Rio Verde (Green river), running directly from north to south, to which the whole plain slants. Immediately along its western bank rises the Sierra Wasatch, forming a continuous mountain barrier toward the west. Opposite the center of this hypothenuse is the gorge of the Sweetwater, enveloping the eastern point of the triangle. The remaining sides extend hence, the one to the northwest, the other to the southwest. Along the former, in length one hundred and nine miles, rises the stupendous mass of the Cordillera known here locally as the 'Wind River Mountains;' along the latter, a similar mass of the Cordillera, but of inferior altitude, known locally as the 'Table Mountains.' The area of the plain of the South Pass is about equivalent to that of New

Jersey. Its surface is of clay, resembling kaolino, of which porcelain is made, and has the absolute smoothness of that material, filtered through water and compacted by pressure. From the three angles of its rim issue the Sweetwater, flowing east into the Platte and to the Atlantic; the Snake river, flowing northwest to Walla-Walla, and thence with the Columbia to the North Pacific; and the Rio Verde, south into the Bay of California—by whose western affluent, also, Black Fork, exists the easiest egress into the basin of the Great Salt Lake.

"Most probably no spot on the globe has grouped into one view so much of intense grandeur in the variety and number of its physical wonders. From a single ice-crowned summit of the Wind River Mountains are seen the gorges of the Missouri, Yellowstone, Platte, Colorado, and Snake rivers, all radiating from its base, and each the equal of the Danube in length and the volume of its waters. Five primary chains of snowy mountains here culminate together to this central apex, from which they radiate out between the rivers—the dorsal mass of the Cordillera reaching toward the north to the Arctic Sea and toward the south to the Antarctic, the Sierra Wasatch, the Snake River chain, the Salmon River Mountains, all crested with snow, and each having an unbroken length of 1,000 miles. The South Pass is 1,400 miles from Astoria; it is the same distance from St. Louis. It is, then, in the middle region of the continent. It is the *only Pass* through the 'mountain formation' from hence as far as the Isthmus of Tehuantepec. From this comes the name South Pass, as being the most *southern Pass* to which you may ascend by an effluent of the Atlantic, and step immediately on to a stream descending uninterruptedly out to the Pacific. This name is as ancient as the Pass itself. Into it concentrate the great trails of the buffalo—geographers and road-makers before the coming of man. The Indian, the Mexican, and the American, successors to one another, have not deflected from the instincts of the buffalo, nor will they whilst the primeval mountains last in their present unshattered bulk. This is the continental highway of the people; through this exclusively millions have already poured to and fro with their children, their free principles, their cattle—assembled in caravans, on foot and mounted, with wagons, hand-carts, knapsacks, and bringing with them their household gods and the tabernacle of civil and religious liberty.

"The South Pass is the *only and exclusively continental Pass*. The outlet at the eastern angle is known as the gorge of the Sweetwater river, which descends to the Platte; that at the northern angle as the gorge of the Grosventre river, which descends to the Snake river. These are both short and slender mountain streams, accomplishing their descent in beds of the extremest sinuosity, but without waterfalls. They both flow from chasms in the flanks of the immense mass of the Wind River Mountains, which here forms an arc, fronting to the west, and issue out upon the plain. But the plain is traversed by a gentle divide, parallel with the mountain, and no more distinguishable than the level given by engineers to any ordinary street. Against this, these two streams are deflected into opposite courses, the former to burrow its way around the arc of the mountain to the southeast, the other toward the northwest. To one who observes this from the plains, there is presented a similar miraculous configuration of the land, such as displays itself to one who, navigating the Propontic Sea, beholds the Dardanelles upon his right hand and the Bosphorus on his left. Moreover, the sky is without clouds and rainless, the atmosphere intensely brilliant, temperate, serene, and encompassed round by scenery of the austerest sublimity. We have seen that the elevation of the South Pass is 7,500 feet, and that Snake river runs continuously out of it, by the most direct and favorable course, 1,400 miles to the Pacific sea, tunneling consecutively the Blue or Salmon River range of mountains, the snowy Andes, and all other transverse ranges and obstructions. Here is, then, an uninterrupted water declination, through and across the whole 'mountain formation,' descending by a plane, dipping five feet to the mile! From the adjacent eastern rim of the plain of the South Pass runs out Sweetwater into the Platte, which, tunneling consecutively all the outlying ranges of the Cordillera of the Sierra Madre, forms a similar uninterrupted water declination, in a very straight line of 1,400 miles to St. Louis, descending by the same average dip of five feet per mile.

"The sciences which delineate and explain to the human

understanding the details of matter, as it fits itself in myriads of millions of variegated forms to fill out the supreme order of the universe, develop nothing so interesting to the heart of civilized man as this sublime fact of physical geography in the supreme engineering of the Creator. This line of gently undulating river grades, girdling the middle zone of our Union from sea to sea, in one smooth, continuous, and unbroken cord, 3,000 miles in length, fitting the isothermal axis of the temperate climates, crossing one river only at St. Louis, and outflanking all the mountains, presents to us the counterpart of that waterline of the Old World, commencing at the extremity of the Euxine, passing down the Mediterranean, and debouching out into the ocean."

The reader will find this brief quotation to be an interesting description of that great continental highway through which millions of the human race will yet pass to and fro in the eager pursuit of wealth and pleasure in the years of the future. It is the only available pathway through which the citizens of the Republic can enter to the Pacific shore.

Leaving the South Pass, we are compelled to go more than six hundred miles south, or to Mexico, before we can find any available pathway across the continent, while north of the South Pass any possible passage is so far away that it will remain unoccupied for generations to come. The consequence is that the great Pacific railway of the continent and the nation must be that which is constructed by way of the South Pass. It will be more direct and more useful, while along its pathway will follow the stream of civilization around the world.

It is now understood that the Omaha or Union Pacific road will be constructed through the South Pass, and the Kansas or Central Pacific road will from the western part of Kansas be directed to Santa Fe, and from thence constructed upon what was formerly known as the southern route to the Pacific. It will be seen at once that this road, when completed, will not, as a Pacific railway, be so valuable to those cities and towns adjacent to its eastern end. To them it will only serve as a way-road to New Mexico, while the great Pacific trade will be done over the railway of the South Pass, which will be the great commercial umbilical cord of the continent.

The Central Pacific Railway, when completed, will be a great continental road, penetrating an empire of country and opening to the two oceans and the Mississippi river a vast commerce, which is yet to be developed in the further and mightier west, but the trade of this road will essentially be continental, while the trade of the Union Pacific or Omaha road will be the great highway over which the trade and commerce of the oriental lands and ours will be done.

Touching, in a higher and broader sense, the change of the action of the commerce of the world which will be effected by these roads when completed, and the expanded growth of empire on this continent, is a part of the subject that cannot be fully comprehended at present; the reality can but vaguely be seen now even by the wisest and most far-reaching minds. To get even the first conception of the final triumphs of progress and commerce to which these great national highways are to lead, we must first contemplate the whole globe girdled with railways by land and steamships by oceans; we must contemplate embracing these lines of steam a vast growth of civilization and commerce, supported by more than one hundred millions of industrious and intelligent American people, struggling for all the successes of life. We must contemplate "one vast confederation, stretching from the frozen north in unbroken line to the glowing south, and from the wild billows of the Atlantic westward to the calmer waters of the Pacific, and behold one people, one law, one language, and one faith, and over all this vast continent the home of freedom." A just comprehension of all these things will give an insight to what these great railways are to unfold for the future.

The present progress of their construction is as rapid as the circumstances will allow. Each line is being pushed forward in a most satisfactory manner. The time for their completion is uncertain, but will probably require from three to five years hence. Every interest, both of capital and commerce, urges the work forward, and not only ours, but other nations and people, wait eagerly for their final completion. Let us hail the day of the final work as a day of immortal event.

Note.—St. Louis has a double interest in the construction of the continental railways. Her immediate interest lies in the prosecution of the main trunk of the Central Pacific road to Denver, and from thence form a connection with the Union Pacific, or Omaha road, and thence by way of the South Pass reach the Pacific shores. Her secondary interest is in the branch extension of the Central Pacific to Albuquerque and to the Pacific coast.

THE GREAT BRIDGE AT ST. LOUIS.

Each age and each nation produces its great works in some phase of civil progress. The early Jews built the tower of Babel; Egypt had the Pyramids and Catacombs; Greece her Parthenon and unequaled temples of worship; Rome had her Coliseum; the middle ages, their walled cities. But modern civilization, passing beyond the age of selfishness, ambition, and idolatry, gives to mankind magnificent structures of greater use as the triumphs of the genius of the race.

The greatest work of mechanical art that the world has yet beheld, is the Crystal Palace of the nineteenth century. It combines in one lovely master-piece, and one glow of associated beauty, the highest civilization and progress of man.

The leading feature of the present age is the strife for commercial dominion. In this department of civilization is enlisted more capital, talent, and men than in any other. All the rapid strides of the race are made in its interest—whether in the achievement of art, of science, or of genius. The wild billows of the Atlantic have been defied by steam and electricity, and the two great continents of kindred shores, united by these subtle agents, and now with one steady grand march does civilization, carried by the tides of men, continue its journey to the west—to the high mountains, and the broad and calmer waters of the wide Pacific ocean. With these great movements come the master works of mechanics and arts.

Since the invention of the steam engine, the railway system may be regarded as the greatest aid to civilization the arts have afforded, on account of the rapid intercommunion of men and ideas, and the exchange of products. But a great and valuable railway system without bridges to cross the inland streams would be an impossibility; hence the remarkable development of genius and art, and the concentration of capital, to construct in ample proportions these master-fabrics for commercial use.

Here, then, is submitted a brief statement of that which is to constitute, when completed, the greatest work of its particular kind that engineering skill has yet given to the world. The work of constructing a great bridge over the Mississippi river at St. Louis, like all other great projects of a public character, has been long attended with difficulties and delays. The want of a sufficiently enterprising public spirit to take hold of the work and command the genius and the capital for its prosecution, has made it a subject of special discussion for many years past. But the growing and pressing demand of the commercial and railroad interest bearing upon St. Louis forced positive action out of the agitation, and charters were procured from the Legislatures of Missouri and Illinois, with ample provisions to secure its construction if sustained by sufficient public spirit. The time for building it seemed to have come. No sooner were the charters procured than the right public spirit was manifest, and men of character and wealth came forward promptly and organized a Company, and proceeded to raise the estimated amount of money necessary, and the work is now under way.

The plan for the bridge submitted by the Chief Engineer of the Company, and which was accepted, will be found of great public interest. It is in some particulars quite original, and perhaps superior to anything of the kind in existence. It provides for crossing the river with a bridge built upon three magnificent arches made of cast-steel. These arches will rest upon two great river piers, and upon two shore piers. Each of these great arches or spans of the bridge will be formed of four ribbed arches of cast-steel, having a rise of about one-tenth of the span. Each of these ribbed arches will in turn be formed of two ribs, eight feet apart, one above the other, and strongly braced between with diagonal steel braces. The center span resting on the great channel pier will be 515 feet in length, and the two side spans will each be 497 feet, making, with the width of the piers, the total length of the bridge, from shore to shore, 1,689 feet. Each end of the bridge will have an extension of five great arch-ways of 30 feet span each, crossing the wharves on each shore. On the St. Louis side, near Washington avenue, the carriage-way will be extended to Third street.

The bridge will have two floors, the upper one being devoted to the use of pedestrians, vehicles, and double tracks for street cars. The lower one will accommodate a double track for the passage of steam cars in each direction. The roadway on the opposite shore will be extended over the two first streets in East St. Louis, and descending with an easy grade, will form a continuation of the stone dyke, on which a fine turnpike road is now made. The entire bridge and approaches will be about 3,700 feet long. The arch-ways are to be of sufficient highth to render no obstruction to the business of the levee.

In ordinary stages of water, there will be from 60 to 70 feet in the clear below the bridge at the central arch. At the center, the lowest part of the bridge will be 50 feet above high water mark; this distance is slightly diminished under the side arches, owing to the fact that a slight curve is given to the bridge in its general construction.

The railway, consisting of a double track, one narrow gauge, four feet 8½ inches, the other wide gauge of six feet, each track having a third rail, which will enable the closest connections with all trains, will be suspended from the iron beams supporting the carriage way, and will rest on trusses or stretchers running the entire length of the bridge. About the middle of the block, between Second and Third streets, the railway will enter a tunnel, extending thence, under Washington avenue, to Ninth street; here the tunnel will curve round into Eleventh street, at Olive, and following Eleventh street to the south side of Clark avenue, will there emerge into the open air, and enter a grand union depot a short distance from the terminus of the tunnel.

The great piers and the mode of their construction is one of the most interesting features of this bridge, and especially when we consider the great depth to be reached to secure a permanent rock foundation, by which to enable them to withstand the combined power of the Mississippi and Missouri rivers, and the ever-changing sands in the bed of the stream. A foundation on the underlying rock alone will secure safety. To reach this, one pier must go down through 20 feet of water and 80 feet of sand. This great pier will, in total hight, be 195 feet, and 100 feet in width at the base, with a breadth tapering from 55 to 30 feet, and will consist of a mass of masonry weighing over 30,000 tons.

The other river pier will pass down through water and sand over 70 feet to the rock foundation below, and with a total highth of 170 feet. This pier will consist of a mass of masonry weighing some 25,000 tons.

All this great mass of masonry must be placed in position within three consecutive months, in a river with a current running four or five miles an hour. To accomplish this, the following plan has been adopted: Around the site of the pier a number of screw piles, 16 inches in diameter, will be sunk. These can be rapidly screwed into the sand. On these piles a strong framework of timber will be erected within, and supported by a huge boiler-iron caisson, well strengthened by angle iron bars placed horizontally around it, about three feet apart, on its inner surface; it will then be put together with screw bolts. This caisson is simply intended to be used as an iron curtain, of an elliptical shape, open at the bottom, and, being considerably larger than the intended pier, will completely surround it. It is not the design to pump the water out of it, and hence it is not braced across from side to side, but is simply designed to exclude the sand. It will be held against the current by chains until it sinks by its own weight in the sand. When it has sunk to a sufficient depth, the work of pumping out the sand is commenced, which will be done with powerful sand-pumps; and as the caisson will be slightly larger at the bottom than at the top, its inclined sides will facilitate its sinking as the sand within is removed. In this way it will finally be sunk to the rock, and, reaching above the surface, will completely inclose the water within. The sand being removed from the rock, a bed of concrete mortar will be spread over the rock and carefully leveled off. This mortar-bed will be one or two feet in thickness above the highest parts of the rock. With this arrangement to receive the piers, a portion of the down-stream end of the caisson will be temporarily removed to admit within it a huge, flat-bottomed boat. This boat will have its bottom constructed of squared timbers, placed solid, and of about 30 inches in thickness and thoroughly calked. It will form the base of the pier, as it is known that wood is practically indestructible under water. The sides of the boat will be nearly vertical, made of strong timber and plank, and calked tight. In this great vessel, the interior of which will be of the size and shape of the intended pier, the masonry work of the pier will be prosecuted as fast as ten or twelve steam hoisting machines and the frame-works above can supply stone and other materials to the masons working within. As the masonry progresses, the boat slowly settles down with its gigantic load, and as it sinks, the sides are built up to exclude the water, and will ultimately reach a highth of 100 feet. It is estimated that when about 40 feet of the pier has been constructed, the boat will have reached the bed prepared for it within the caisson, and will then rest upon the rock. The masonry will be built up rapidly; the massive stones being thoroughly grouted, course after course, with hydraulic cement, until the structure of the pier finally emerges above the surface of the water. The sides of the boat will be secured to its bottom by screws, which can be loosened from the top; and when the stone work has reached above the surface, the boat will be permitted to fill with water, and the screws will be disengaged and the sides taken out. The next step will be to remove the iron caisson. The screws supporting it will be put in motion, and it will be drawn up from the sand, unbolted, and removed, to be used in the construction of the other pier. The further removal of all preparations for building at once follows, and this new marine monster of art is left for all time to brave the ice and other aggressions of the Father of Waters.

This constitutes a brief outline description of the great St. Louis Railway and Passenger Bridge, which is now in process of construction, and will require at least three years for its completion, and an estimated expenditure of $5,000,000.

A very brief classification of the approved bridges of the day, and an allusion to specimens of the various kinds, will, perhaps, enable the casual reader to receive a better impression of the magnitude of the St. Louis bridge. There are four prominent styles of bridges, which are generally adopted by the engineering profession, when they aim to erect something that will endure to remote generations. The tubular, the suspension, the lattice, and the arch—all constructed of iron, in one or more of its forms. The tubular, invented by Robert Stephenson, although materially aided by Fairbairn, will always, we think, be regarded as one of the great ideas of the nineteenth century. It is a straight, hollow, rectangular tube. The Britannia bridge is the grandest specimen; for its longest span, or reach, between supports, is 450 feet. But long as it is, it was lifted in one piece 100 feet high, to its present position. The Victoria bridge has no span of equal length, nor was it elevated in the same way.

The suspension, in its crude forms, is of ancient date. It is found in all lands, but until later years it has never received the indorsement of engineers as the reliable support of railway trains; and in this respect, it can hardly be said to have thoroughly disarmed sound criticism, when we claim we are building something that is truly permanent. It possesses some qualities that will always render it popular. It can be constructed more easily in many positions. A much greater span can be obtained than by any other known method — and the cost is comparatively less. Perhaps this last feature can be understood, when we remember that the Niagara bridge, with a span of 821 feet, was built for less than the yearly interest on the sum expended on the Britannia bridge. Its general construction is well known. In Europe, the prominent specimens are the Menai, by Telford, with a span of 580 feet, and the Freyburg, in Switzerland, with a span of 870 feet. In this country, Ellet and Roebling have identified themselves with the Wheeling, Niagara, Cincinnati, and other bridges. Ellet constructed the Wheeling bridge, 1,000 feet span, which failed to withstand the winds; yet Mr. Ellet was a great man. Mr. Roebling may be regarded as the great exponent of the suspension bridge in this country. His reputation may well be envied; for while the great engineers of Europe were saying it was impossible, he went on with the Niagara bridge; and now, after fifteen years' successful usage, it has caused the engineers of the old world to reverse their theories.

He has just completed the Cincinnati bridge, and if, in future times, the suspension shall have become recognized as a thoroughly safe, permanent structure for railway trains, to Mr. Roebling, more than any other, will the credit belong.

The lattice bridge has been and is now a very popular type of bridge. The name will readily convey a correct impression of its general construction. In some respects it is preferable to the tubular. It is less costly, and is less rigid, which some claim to be an advantage. As fine a specimen of this kind, perhaps, as can be seen anywhere, is at Cologne, over the Rhine. Its longest reach is 330 feet. It is, however, liable to oscillation.

But yielding everything to the suspension and the lattice that can with reason be claimed for them, it is questionable whether they possess the elements of perpetuity equally with the arch. We know arch bridges have endured for centuries—we do not yet know how long a railway suspension, tubular, or lattice bridge will continue.

The first cast-iron arch bridge was built in 1779, with a span of 100 feet. Many other iron arch bridges have been successfully constructed. They have always been highly esteemed for their strength and durability. The great drawback, perhaps, has been an inability to construct them with a span so wide as to compare favorably with those of other styles. In England, the largest is the Southwark, with a span of 240 feet, and a rise of twenty-four feet. Note this fact, and remember the length of the Britannia, 459 feet, and the length of the Cologne, 330 feet, and then the importance of the St. Louis bridge, with its span of 515 feet, will appear.

Its form is as enduring as any tested by the experience of ages. Its size surpasses that of any, when we consider the true comparison, the length of span. Its material, cast-steel, is the best in the world, ranking with wrought-iron in the ratio of two to one.

The importance of the St. Louis bridge is still further increased when we consider its foundations, their depth, their mode of construction, and the attendant difficulties.

Other engineers of great eminence have proposed the erection of bridges of greater span than this, but it rarely occurs that the location and conditions of the case justify, as in this one, such bold grasp of mind on the part of the engineer, with the no less important accompaniment of a proper manifestation of public spirit on the part of capitalists to carry out his design.

Mr. Latrobe, a noted engineer of Baltimore, has expressed his opinion upon the construction of a bridge at St. Louis. He favored the use of piers higher than those of the present plan, requiring a stationary engine to draw the cars from either side to the center in passing over. He also advocated the use of spans 400 and 500 feet in length.

That modern engineers are anticipating something altogether superior to the past achievements, the following remarks of Mr. Roebling are evidence. He says: "It was left to modern engineering, by the application of the principle of suspension, and by the use of wrought-iron, to solve the problem of spanning large rivers without intermediate supports. Cast and wrought-iron arches, of 100 feet and more, have been quite successful. Nor can it be said that the limit of arching has been reached. Timber arches of much greater span have stood for years, and have rendered good service in this country as well as on the continent of Europe. It is worthy of notice, however, and to be cited as a curious professional circumstance, that the best form of material, so profusely applied by nature in her elaborate constructions, has never been used in arching, although proposed on several occasions. This form is unquestionably the cylindrical, combined in small sections, as is illustrated by vegetable and animal structures. Where strength is to be combined with lightness and elegance, nature never wastes heavy, cumbrous masses. The architects of the middle ages fully illustrated this by their beautiful buttresses and flying arches, combinations of strength and stability, executed with the least amount of material.

"The wrought-iron pipe, now manufactured of all sizes and in such great perfection, offers to the engineer a material for arching which cannot be excelled. A wire cable, composed of an assemblage of wires, constitutes the best catenary arch for the suspension of great weights; and, as a parallel to this, if the catenary is reversed, the best upright arch for the support of a bridge may be formed by an assemblage of wrought-iron pipes, of one and a half or two inches diameter or more. Arches of 1,000 feet span and more may be rendered practicable and safe upon this system. I venture to predict that the two great rival systems of future bridge engineering will be the inverted and upright arch; the former made of wire, and the latter of pipe, both systems rendered stable by the assistance of lattice work, or by stays, trusses, and girders."

It has already been stated that the bridge to be built at St. Louis is to be made of cast-steel; and in the meantime, extensive experiments will be made to thoroughly test the strength of the metal, and no possible precaution will be neglected or effort omitted to make this bridge a complete and perfect success, for it is the general conviction that when built, it will be the greatest and most magnificent structure of the kind in the world. Although not so great in length as the Victoria bridge over the St. Lawrence, which is nearly two miles long, nor the bridge over the Nebudda, in India, which is one and a half miles long, nor the bridge from Bassein to the main land, which is over three miles long, yet its magnificent spans and stately piers place it far above these bridges in character and structure. And when once built, it will be grander than the Colossus at Rhodes, grander than the Pharos at Alexandria. It will vitalize the commerce of the Mississippi Valley, and unite the great railway chain between New York and San Francisco. When completed, it will place the name of its builder with that of Telford, Smeaton, Stephenson, and other distinguished engineers of the world. Mr. Eads already stands prominent as one of the most enterprising and public-spirited citizens of St. Louis; and should this bridge enterprise, in which he is more prominent than any other, prove successful, his character and reputation will become the public property of the country, even as the bridge itself will be. Almost proverbial for the invariable success attending everything he undertakes, and with a world-wide reputation for practical ingenuity and indomitable energy, we hail his prominent identification with this work as an assurance of its successful completion. To him, and to the enlightened, public-spirited citizens who have pledged their capital and influence to sustain the enterprise, will justly belong the glory that will surely attach to the St. Louis Bridge.

SPECIAL TO ST. LOUIS.

One of the strongest incentives of human nature is that which impels man to seek for happiness and success. The means of happiness are diligently sought for through every science, through art, and through industry, and each year adds new contributions to some phase of society.

It has been the pride and distinguishing characteristic of mankind, in all times, to adorn and beautify their great cities, and provide facilities for commerce and pleasure for the populace.

Thebes, the pride of Egypt, and the first metropolis of arts and sciences, was distinguished for its hundred gates—Baalbec for its gigantic temples, "the ruins of which baffle the imagination of man."

Babylon had her wonderful walls and her hanging gardens; Nineveh her unequaled carvings, and Persepolis her world of palaces. So in modern times, each city is slowly advancing with improvements that confer privileges and benefits upon its citizens. The certainty of a wonderful future for St. Louis urges the necessity for such steps to be taken by her citizens as will insure the most liberal facilities for her business interest, and the most advanced improvements possible to secure health, pleasure, and the higher culture of her people. What she is to-day ought not to be, and cannot be, the city of the future. Her people of this year, and of this generation, will not do their duty, if they, too, do not distinguish themselves—if they do not make the beginning of such improvements as will be finished by those of coming generations. Without generalizing the improvements necessary to great cities, it is proper to notice especially those which ought to be made for St. Louis.

A city ought, by all means, to be abundantly supplied with water, to the extent that each citizen will have no difficulty in getting all the water needed. To expend money in a project that does not answer the demands for which it is designed is wrong. Competent engineers should be employed, and ample and permanent provisions for water be made. Good water and good air are indispensable to the welfare and health and happiness of a great city, and both should be provided.

Another matter of great importance to which a city should be earnestly devoted, is to make such improvements and provisions as will facilitate its business interest. This must be done by wise municipal legislation—by protecting health, making public improvements, and aiding private enterprise, to facilitate the travel of the business man from his home to his place of business. It is becoming evident in our great cities, that the ordinary mode of city travel, by street cars and the omnibus, is not fast enough to answer the business demands of the people; consequently, each city is looking out for some improvement in speed. The too frequent stopping of cars to take on and let off passengers, causes great loss of time to the business man, especially if he lives at a great distance. Various efforts have been made to overcome this difficulty, but no plan has been found sufficiently satisfactory to warrant its adoption. The city of London has partially adopted the underground travel, which meets with tolerable success. But the expense and inconvenience of such a mode renders it insufficient. What is required, is speed and safety. Speed cannot be obtained by the use of horses, nor is the use of steam safe in our streets, under the present regulations. Yet speed and safety must be obtained sooner or later. The necessity for many of the population and business men to live at a distance, and the greater desire of more to live away in the country, will soon require quicker transit.

The close connection of the travel in a city with the beauty of its arrangement, and the pleasure it affords, necessarily ally the two interests, and what is necessary for one will contribute to the other.

In prospect of the future greatness of St. Louis, it must be conceded that the largest provisions should be made for broad and extensive avenues and immense parks. To make ample provisions in this direction, there should be three great avenues extending from the river, or at least from Fourth street, in a straight line, west, to the city limits or beyond. To provide these avenues, the city ought to purchase, and cause to be vacated, certain entire tiers of blocks, and such other grounds as are necessary, to extend the avenues beyond the city limits, viz: The ground between Wash and Carr streets, and between Market and Walnut streets, and such an enlargement of Chouteau avenue as to make it equal to the two above; and by this means open out three great avenues, which, when properly improved, would furnish ample room for safe and speedy transit to the distant homes, besides furnishing the city with three great avenues, such as she needs and ought to have. Such avenues, when adorned with trees and shrubbery of beauty and value, and flowing water, would add infinitely to the worth and goodness and greatness of St. Louis. In addition to these, let Grand avenue be thoroughly improved, and extended to the river above and below, so as to encircle thus much of the city. Still more, three large parks ought to be provided and improved in magnificent style.

With these large and splendid avenues, steam transit could be used with safety and speed, and thus meet all the demands for rapid traveling; and thousands who now are, and henceforth would be compelled to live in the narrow limits of the city, would make homes in the airy suburbs of the country. Some arrangement of this kind must, sooner or later, be made—the public and private interest of the citizens will demand it. Cities are under a moral obligation to provide for the health and comfort of their poor, and not only must they be furnished with good water and air, but public parks, and other places, must be fitted up for Sunday resort, for the thousands who are confined indoors at honest toil during the week.

With such improvements will come the higher institutions of civilized life—temples of music, halls of science, palaces of art, and studios for genius.

There are those who will judge these views extravagant, and the improvements impossible, but they are within the legitimate scope of improvements which St. Louis ought to make, in view of her future greatness.

The whole project is deserving of consideration, and ought to be publicly considered and acted upon. It is high time that something great and valuable—of more than ordinary concern—was projected for a city of such immense possibilities, even with the hopeful assurance of being the seat of national empire.

Not only would the citizens of this generation heartily rejoice in such magnificent improvements, but millions yet to come, with footsteps soft as those who now tread her walks, and with music notes of sweeter tones, and aspirations of higher aims, would rejoice with fuller hearts, and adorn with more tender hands the great works that this people had given to them.

THE EXPENSE, AND HOW TO MEET IT.

It is easy to imagine that there are those whose selfishness will not allow them to consent to such extended improvements at the public expense, even if they should happen to be impressed with their excellency. But who is there so short-sighted that he cannot see that the very moment those avenues are opened, and well-regulated public conveyance provided to their farthest extent, St. Louis will stand as the most princely city of the world, far-famed for her wonderful and proud public improvements?

Grant that the expense for the purchase of the grounds for the avenues and parks, and their improvements, reaches $30,000,000, which would probably be an over-estimate. The city, with a vigorous administration of her public affairs, could make the purchase without a hazard of her financial interests. When the prosecution of the work is determined upon, let her appoint competent agents, to go ten miles or more into the country, and purchase, as near the terminus of these avenues as possible, ten thousand or more acres of land, which shall be held by the city, and improved, and sold at advanced prices from year to year, for suburban and country residences. By this means the city could raise a considerable portion of the money to pay for the purchase of the avenues. With the avenues purchased, and improved for at least ten miles in the country, or to the new grounds, let there be constructed the improved means of conveyance, as follows: Erect one row of iron posts of sufficient size, and from 12 to 15 feet high, and say from 12 to 15 feet distant from each other, except at the crossings of the streets, where the distance can be made greater. These posts must be firmly planted in the center, and extend the entire length of each avenue. At the top end of each post attach arms, or a cross-bar, whereon to lay the railing for the new road. Then, with a light engine, and perhaps improved motive power and light cars, each one being capable of carrying two thousand pounds, trains can be run with as great speed and as much safety as they now run on any of the roads traversing the country, and thousands of mechanics and business men can then go as easily ten miles from the city, where there is pure air, cheap rents, and good water, as they now go two miles.

The too frequent stopping to take on and let off passengers can be overcome by having depots at intervals.

These new roads, once built, would yield an immense income to the city, besides furnishing better and cheaper travel. In other parts of the city the street travel must be confined to the alleys; the present mode is fast becoming very objectionable.

Those avenues, when once opened, should be well improved with shrubbery, walks, and fountains.

Again, let the city levy an additional tax on all property each side of the avenues, for the purpose of aiding to pay the bonded indebtedness made for their purchase. There can be no just objection against this, for it is a common mode of raising funds, for a special purpose, in all cities.

By these three channels of income, from the lands in the country, the railroads, and the additional taxation, the debt for the whole purchase and improvement of parks and avenues could be paid in twenty years. The income would not fall far short of the two mill tax on the Illinois Central Railroad.

By this plan the city could very well afford to engage in such magnificent improvements, even if they cost $50,000,000.

NOTE.—This pamphlet is not written in the special interest of St. Louis, but in the interest of the NATION. And in so far as it falls short of being essentially a national pamphlet, the failure is justly attributed to two causes—

I. An inability to comprehend the facts and apply them in their true relations.

II. An inability to get many facts and statistics desired, both from the Pacific Slope and other quarters of the country.

The allusions made to St. Louis as the city destined to control the seat of empire in the Republic, are because she is already a great central city, forming a nucleus around which an expanding commerce will revolve, and a great Republic grow. All the facts point to her as the great inland city of the continent, and as holding the available position for the capital of the nation.

But in indicating what the facts seem to warrant, it is not meant to cast a selfish reflection against Chicago, or any other city of the country. In short, it is narrow foolishness for the citizens of Chicago and St. Louis to be jealous and envious of each other's prosperity and industry, for in the Great West is ample room for both cities to reach a point of growth unequaled in human history. There never will be a time when there is not enough of room for both of them, occupying the places they now do, and never a time when the interest of the one is not the interest of the other, and the growth of one aided by the growth of the other.

Let each one learn that her true interests are best served by an enterprising industry, guided by liberality and a comprehensive conception of the rapidly advancing tide of progress. Without these, written essays in favor of either will be of no avail, and in the face of these, jealousy and envy are unbecoming the dignity of the citizens of either.

www.ingramcontent.com/pod-product-compliance
Lightning Source LLC
Chambersburg PA
CBHW020120170426
43199CB00009B/576